CW00890464

TAOIST
WISDOM

TAOIST WISDOM

Daily Teachings from the Taoist Sages

TIMOTHY FREKE

A GODSFIELD BOOK

First published in Great Britain in 1999
by Godsfield Press Ltd
A division of David and Charles Ltd
Laurel House, Station Approach,
New Alresford, Hants SO24 9JY, UK

10 9 8 7 6 5 4 3 2 1

Designed for Godsfield Press by
The Bridgewater Book Company

Printed and bound in Hong Kong

ISBN 1-899434-74-7

Picture research by Caroline Thomas
Design: Alison Honey

The publishers wish to thank the following for the use of pictures:

Original artwork: Peter Cavacuti pp.10, 15,17, 28, 34,40, 47,

55, 64, 73, 83, 98, 105, 110, 117, 120

CONTENTS

INTRODUCTION

People mistakenly seek for the truth in books which necessarily only contain false ideas.

CHUANG TZU

A book on Tao is a profound paradox. Books are only a collection of words that lack the power ever to elucidate the enigma of Tao. Tao is a living reality that must be entered into. It is thoughts and opinions that blind us to Tao. Anything we say about Tao is necessarily misleading, because it is only when we step beyond language into the immediacy of experience in the here and now that Tao becomes obvious.

TEACHING US TO UNLEARN

The great Taoist sage, Lao Tzu, tells us categorically, "If you think you can speak about Tao, it is clear you don't know what you're talking about." Yet this does not stop him attempting to communicate his extraordinary teachings. However, like all of the Taoist sages, he does not intend his teachings to be taken as dogmas which rigidly define the truth, or absolute moral codes to keep us on the straight and narrow. They are evocative insights that point beyond words to a silent experience of enlightenment. They are not designed to teach us anything, but to help us unlearn all the artificial ideas we have accrued in the process of social conditioning. They encourage us to awaken our natural, intuitive understanding of life and our place within it. As Lao Tzu explains, "Someone seeking learning knows more and more, but someone seeking Tao knows less and less – until things just are what they are."

THE GREAT TAOIST MASTERS

This book contains a wealth of wisdom that can nurture this process of awakening. It draws primarily on the ancient Taoist classics attributed to the famous sages Lao Tzu, Chuang Tzu, and Lieh Tzu, probably written in the fifth and fourth centuries B.C.E. There is much scholarly debate about whether these works were really composed by these authors or, indeed, whether these individuals ever actually existed. But this need not concern us here. What matters for us are the teachings themselves.

TAOIST RELIGION

As invariably happens, centuries after these living masters (whoever they may have been), Taoism became formalized and degenerated into religious ritual and superstition. The great sages, such as Lao Tzu, became treated like celestial gods, to be worshiped and petitioned with prayers. Taoists began to practice complex spiritual disciplines that promised magical powers, longevity, or even immortality. This has little to do with the Taoism of the ancient masters. Indeed, they are completely hostile to such religious formalities and esoteric practices, emphasizing instead the need for complete naturalness.

CONFUCIUS

Alongside Taoism there developed in China an influential rival philosophy originating in the teachings of K'ung Fu Tzu, better known in the West as Confucius. Witnessing the disintegration of the society in which he lived, Confucius sought to return people to the traditional rites and rituals practiced by their ancestors, which were being abandoned and forgotten. This concern with culture rather than Nature was antithetical to Taoists, who often ridiculed Confucius for his pompous formality. Some say that at the end of his life Confucius saw the error of his ways and became a Taoist, but this is probably only a legend created by Taoists so that they could claim this extremely popular sage as one of their own. The quotes from Confucius in this book are those attributed to him by Taoists and are not representative of orthodox Confucianism.

FOOD FOR THOUGHT

The thought-for-the-day format of the book offers the opportunity to embark on an unfolding adventure into the paradoxical world of the Taoist sages. Day by day we can begin to catch their deceptively simple vision of life. We can unlearn our anxiety, our need to control, our presumption that we know what life is, our fear of death and change – all the opinions and prejudices we have inherited from our culture. Under the influence of their relentless compassion we can begin instead to celebrate the incomprehensible splendor of existence, to flow with the constant tides of Yin and Yang, to merge our separate identities in the great ocean of Tao.

JOURNEY TO THE CENTER

This book is not some sort of curriculum. Although it is arranged in topics to aid comprehension, there is no set order in which these teachings need to be contemplated. Taoist philosophy is like a circle. It doesn't matter where you start, it will lead you around and around, until you realize that what is really important is the still center of the circle that you are circumambulating. It does not matter how you approach this book, or where you start, or if you finish. You may like to begin by reading the introductory paragraphs which begin each topic to give yourself an overview of Taoism, and then take a quote each day as a focus for meditation. You may like to read it from cover to cover or to focus intensely on a certain topic. You may like to simply browse through the book until something particularly strikes you. Approach it as you want to. This is the Taoist way. If you do, it may succeed in reminding you of that innate understanding of life that was already yours when you were too young to even think.

THE ONENESS OF TAO

The Chinese word "Tao" literally means "way." Tao is the way it is – the ultimate reality. The Taoist sages teach that all separate things actually form a great Whole. This all-subsuming totality is Tao. It can not be described in any particular way, because it is everything. It is what IS. Yet Tao should not be pictured as some monolithic "One Thing." Tao is not a thing at all. Tao is a process of constant change. It is the way life works. Perhaps the English word that best conveys the meaning of Tao is "Nature." Just as modern science sees the ever-changing physical universe as a creation of the changeless abstract laws of Nature, so the ancient Taoist sages saw Tao as an abstract permanence that expresses itself as concrete flux. Tao is the all-encompassing Nature that underlies and creates the individual natures of all things. Tao is all that exists, but it is also the nothingness from which everything comes. It is the unfolding of being from non-being. Tao unites all opposites and resolves all paradoxes. It is that which can never be comprehended by the rational mind. "Tao" is an inadequate name for an impossible idea. It is a way of pointing to the ineffable Mystery.

道牛

JANUARY

Mysteriously existing before Heaven and Earth.
Silent and empty.
An unchanging Oneness.
An everchanging presence.
The Mother of all Life.
Without wishing to define it, I say it is "The Whole."
It is impossible to really give it a name, but I call it "Tao."

LAO TZU

JANUARY

Tao is the Whole,
The essential reality.

CHUANG TZU

道牛

JANUARY

You can't see it because it has no form.
You can't hear it because it makes no noise.
You can't touch it because it has no substance.
It cannot be known in these ways,
because it is the all-embracing Oneness.

LAO TZU

JANUARY

If you could apply attributes to Tao
it would not be Tao.

CHUANG TZU

JANUARY

Tao is indefinable original totality.
Ideas create the appearance of separate things.
Always hidden, it is the mysterious essence.
Always manifest, it is the outer appearances.
Essence and appearance are the same.
Only ideas make them seem separate.

LAO TZU

道牛

JANUARY

Words are limited, like the beings that use them, and can only express the affairs of this limited world. They can not be used to describe the eternal, limitless Tao.

TAI GONG DIAO

JANUARY

If you think you can speak about Tao,
it is clear you don't know what you're talking about.

LAO TZU

JANUARY

Indefinable yet continually present.
It is nothing at all.
It is the formless form.
The imageless image.
It can't be grasped by the imagination.
It has no beginning and no end.
This is the essence of Tao.
Stay in harmony with this ancient presence,
and you will know the fullness
of each present moment.

LAO TZU

道牛

JANUARY

Tao is like the ocean.
All rivers run to the ocean without filling it up.
All water comes from it without ever emptying it.

ZHUN MANG

JANUARY

Tao is like an empty space that can never be filled up.
Yet it contains everything:
Blunt and sharp,
resolved and confused,
bright and dull,
the whole of Creation.
Hidden, but always present.
Who created it?
It existed before the Creator.

LAO TZU

JANUARY

Tao flows endlessly like water.
It is there at the beginning and the end.
It is wind rising,
clouds condensing,
thunder rumbling
and rain falling.
It is everything at once.

LAO TZU

JANUARY

Tao is like the axle of a wheel that doesn't turn itself but allows a carriage to travel thousands of miles.

LAO TZU

JANUARY

Tao acts like a still axis
around which the universe evolves.

TAI GONG DIAO

JANUARY

To find the most precious of pearls doesn't compare to discovering the Source of all things.

LAO TZU

JANUARY

Tao is the father-mother of each being,
which it continually creates, dissipates,
and recreates as another being.

CHUANG TZU

JANUARY

Oh Tao!
Who gives to all beings what they require
without claiming to be equitable;
who eternally performs good works,
without claiming to be charitable;
who existed before the beginning,
without claiming to be venerable;
who embraces and supports the universe,
without claiming to be powerful.
It is in You that I move.

XU YOU

JANUARY

The essence of Tao is mystery.

GUANG CHENG

YIN AND YANG

The Oneness of Tao expresses itself as a fundamental duality which the Chinese call "Yin" and "Yang." The dynamic relationship between Yin and Yang creates the appearance of many things from the potentiality of the Oneness. Just as the positive and negative poles on a battery interact to create electricity, so Yin and Yang interact to create life. Yin and Yang express themselves in all opposites: in day and night, male and female, up and down, hot and cold, life and death, something and nothing. Although Yin and Yang are irreconcilable opposites, they are also indivisible complementaries. They only exist together. They are like two ends of one piece of string. They are conceptually separate but intrinsically connected. It is understanding this which enables the Taoist sages to see beyond the appearance of separate things created by Yin and Yang to the essential Oneness of Tao.

18

JANUARY

The Oneness of Tao
expresses itself
as Yin and Yang.

TAI GONG DIAO

JANUARY

Yin and Yang
reciprocally create, destroy, and recreate each other.
From their interaction comes the physical world
with its seasons that produce and destroy each other,
the human world of good and bad,
desirable and undesirable,
prosperity and adversity,
security and danger,
and the distinction between the sexes
with their mutual attraction for procreation.

TAI GONG DIAO

JANUARY

The union of Yin and Yang is the eternal pattern for the copulation of husband and wife that causes procreation, and the mingling of Heaven and Earth through which everything receives life.

CHUANG TZU

JANUARY

The relationship between Yin and Yang
produces a circular evolution
in which every end is a beginning.

TAI GONG DIAO

JANUARY

If you think you can have good without evil,
right without wrong, order without chaos,
you understand nothing about the laws of the universe.
You cannot have Heaven without Earth.
Yin and Yang only exist together.

CHUANG TZU

JANUARY

If everything is one in the universal Tao,
it must simultaneously embrace all the opposites –
including good and evil

CHUANG TZU

24
JANUARY

Something can be beautiful if something else is ugly.
Someone can be good if someone else is bad.
Presence and absence.
Short and long.
High and low.
Before and after.
Gibberish and meaning.
They can only exist together!

LAO TZU

JANUARY

Contentment and resentment.
Pleasure and pain.
Hopes and regrets.
Feelings and thoughts.
Action and repose.
These opposites are sounds
from the same instrument –
fleeting forms of the universal Being.

MASTER QI

JANUARY

Some things are called beautiful and others ugly,
but this is an abuse of words.
Everything is impermanent.
Something that is now beautiful
will metamorphose into something ugly,
and that which is ugly will become beautiful.

THE YELLOW EMPEROR

JANUARY

When things fully flourish they begin to decline.
At midday the sun starts to set.
When the moon is done waxing it starts to wane.
When happiness ends, sadness begins.

LAO TZU

JANUARY

Tao seems to have two aspects
– Yin and Yang –
but actually is never divided.

CHUANG TZU

JANUARY

All opposites are one.
There is in reality
neither truth nor error,
yes or no.
No distinctions
whatsoever.

CHUANG TZU

JANUARY

The enlightened see things from a point of view where this and that, yes and no, still seem indistinct from each other. They see from the still center of the wheel of change. Just as seeing from a distance makes things blur into one, from the enlightened perspective everything is a part of the undifferentiated primal unity.

CHUANG TZU

JANUARY

Gain and loss,
joy and sorrow,
good and bad –
these are all manmade concepts.
To be one with the Oneness
you must be free of duality.

LIEH TZU

道牛

FEBRUARY

FEBRUARY

To live in communion with the author of all beings,
you must place yourself at a time
before Heaven and Earth were separated.

CONFUCIUS

THE BEING OF ALL BEINGS

Tao is the Oneness which appears as diversity. It is Being which expresses itself as all separate beings – including ourselves. Tao is the one Universal Self at the heart of every individual self. Our separate identities are only transitory manifestations of the one Universal Self which is our deeper nature. We are individual expressions of omnipresent Tao. Individual selves live and die, but the Universal Self exists beyond time. Tao has no end, because it has no beginning. Separate individuals are like passing waves on the vast sea of Tao. They rise and fall, appearing to have autonomous existence for a moment, and then returning to the Oneness. But everywhere and forever in reality there is only the ocean.

FEBRUARY

Tao is the Being that resides in all beings.

TAI GONG DIAO

FEBRUARY

Tung-kuo Tzu asked Chuang Tzu, *"Where is Tao to be found?"*. *"It is everywhere,"* replied Chuang Tzu. *"Can you be more specific, please?"* Tung-kuo Tzu insisted. *"It's in an ant,"* said Chuang Tzu. *"Is it so insignificant?"* asked the astonished Tung-kuo Tzu. *"It's in a weed,"* asserted Chuang Tzu. *"Why, that's even more insignificant!"* exclaimed Tung-kuo Tzu. *"It's in broken pottery,"* continued Chuang Tzu. *"Still more insignificant!"* said Tung-kuo Tzu, shaking his head. *"It's in excrement and urine,"* announced Chuang Tzu triumphantly. Tung-kuo Tzu gave no response. *"Sir,"* said Chuang Tzu, *"your question doesn't go to the heart of the matter. When you test the fatness of a pig at market you always look closely at those parts that are less and less likely to be fat. Do the same with Tao and you will find that it is not in any particular thing, because it is in everything."*

FEBRUARY

All things have their individual natures.
Tao is that which unites
all natures into one Nature.
It is not one thing or another
but is in all things equally.

HAN FEI TZU

道牛

5

FEBRUARY

Tao expresses itself as the multiplicity of beings.

CHUANG TZU

FEBRUARY

The only word to describe the state before time when everything was One is the general verb "being."

CHUANG TZU

FEBRUARY

What can one say of universal Being except IT IS?

CHUANG TZU

FEBRUARY

The universe is the body of one Being.

LAO TZU

FEBRUARY

Tao creates and transforms,
takes on form and becomes alive,
develops sentience and acquires intelligence,
acts and sleeps,
but remains always itself –
the cosmic Oneness without differentiation.

LIEH TZU

10

FEBRUARY

All distinct beings are temporarily differentiated from the Whole, and their destiny is to return again to the Whole, which has always been their essential Nature.

CHUANG TZU

FEBRUARY

Heaven and Earth will one day end, just as I will – if you can call a change of state an end! Only Tao, from which everything else originates, will have no end, since it has no beginning.

LIEH TZU

FEBRUARY

Light is born of darkness.
Forms are born of the undifferentiated.
The universal Self
that is expressed in all particular selves
is born of Tao.

LAO TZU

FEBRUARY

To follow Tao,
look within
and return
to the universal Self.

LAO TZU

FEBRUARY

During deep sleep the soul is no longer distracted and is absorbed into unity. During wakefulness, it becomes distracted and distinguishes between diverse beings.

MASTER QI

FEBRUARY

This is joy –
to witness the evolving Tao
expressing itself
as Heaven and Earth
and all beings.

CHUANG TZU

FEBRUARY

Oh Tao!
It makes me supremely happy
to know that I was born from You
and on death will return to You,
that resting I express your Yin nature
and acting I express your Yang nature.

CHUANG TZU

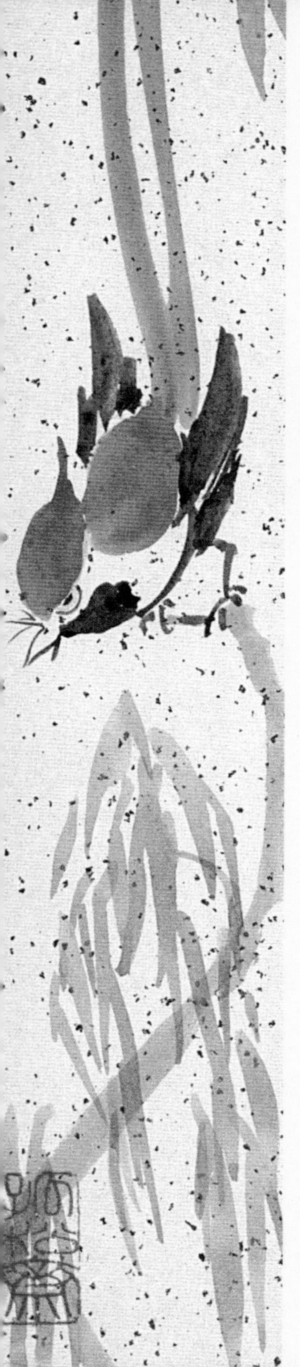

NO SEPARATE INDIVIDUALS

Within the world of appearances created by the duality of Yin and Yang, we experience ourselves as distinct individuals and everything else as "other." This seems to be an irreconcilable opposition, since we can never be anyone else or anything else. Yet without the rest of creation we could not exist. Without air, water, and food we could not live. Without other human beings we would have no sense of our particular identity. Without our parents and their parents, and their parents before them, we would never have been born. Although we think of ourselves as separate and discrete, we are actually an indivisible part of the Whole, reaching back to the dawn of time. All is One. When we see through the illusion of separateness, we understand that "you" and "me" are just ripples on the waters of Tao. All that stands between us and this supreme realization is our habitual idea of ourselves as a separate person. This is why the Taoist sages encourage us to drown ourselves in the great Whole, until we don't even have an "I."

道牛

FEBRUARY

There are no real individuals as such.
Only different expressions of Tao.

CHUANG TZU

FEBRUARY

Reality is an eternal present.
It is as an essential unity
in which there is not even a "you" and a "me."

YONG CHENG

FEBRUARY

Merging their consciousness with the Light and their body with the universe, in luminous emptiness the enlightened experience no-self. Forever detached, they enjoy the play of Heaven and Earth, without intervening through desire or fear, allowing every dilemma to arrive spontaneously at its natural solution.

ZHUN MANG

FEBRUARY

When there is no "other,"
then there is no "I."

CHUANG TZU

道牛

FEBRUARY

The enlightened no longer have an "I,"
for they have united all the parts
in ecstatic contemplation of the One.

CHUANG TZU

FEBRUARY

"You" and "me" are just different points of view.

CHUANG TZU

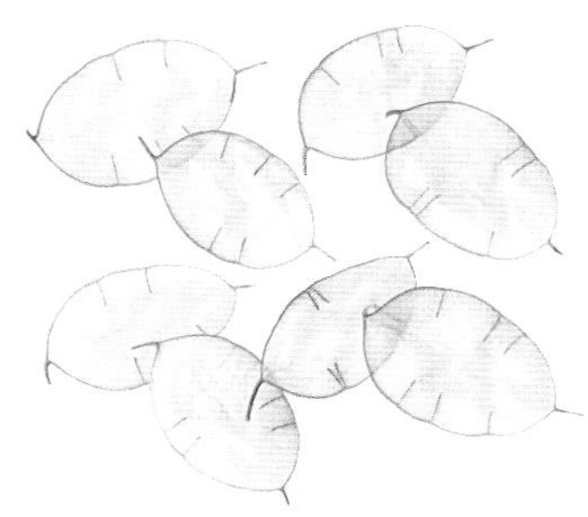

FEBRUARY

Stop identifying with your personality
and see all beings as yourself.

LAO TZU

FEBRUARY

There are two ways of looking at beings;
either as distinct individuals
or as all one in Tao.

CONFUCIUS

FEBRUARY

Fulfillment comes from selflessness.

LAO TZU

FEBRUARY

The only effective remedy for suffering
consists in abandoning everything,
including your own self,
and uniting with Tao.

YI LIAO

FEBRUARY

Imagine being in a boat on a river when another boat collides with you. If that boat was empty, even an irritable person would not lose their temper. Now suppose there was someone in the boat and you shouted to them to keep clear, but they did not listen, although you called out a number of times. Then an argument would certainly ensue. In the first case there was no anger. In the second there was. This is because in the first case the boat was empty and in the second it was occupied. And so it is with us. If we could only pass empty through life, who would want to injure us?

CHUANG TZU

FEBRUARY

Let your body fall away like old clothing.
Let go of your relationships.
Drown yourself in the great Whole.
Abandon your will and your cleverness.
Annihilate yourself through abstraction
until you don't even have an "I."

HONG MENG

FEBRUARY

Although the enlightened inhabit the body of a human being, they are no longer human beings. That which makes them still human is infinitely small compared to the infinite greatness of that through which they are at one with Heaven.

CHUANG TZU

道 牛

MARCH

It is through the power of the impersonal transcendent Self that I affect my listeners. It does not suffer from all the unpleasant character traits belonging to the personal self of the body that is called "Confucius."

CONFUCIUS

MARCH

Outwardly evolve along with everything else.
Inwardly know your true Being
which remains forever the same.

LAO TZU

MARCH

Neither life nor death
bring any changes
to the Self.

LAO TZU

MARCH

The Wise smile at both premature death and excessive old age. They smile, and wish you to smile also, at the changing fortunes of life. For they know that all individual beings are just parts of one evolving Whole.

CHUANG TZU

NO-DOER

The fate of a wave as it rises and falls does not depend on its free choices, but on its predetermined relationship with the currents of the whole sea. The Taoist sages see all individual beings like waves on the ocean of Tao. They therefore understand that we also are not autonomous individuals, but vehicles through which Tao expresses its Nature. From the enlightened perspective we are not the doer of our actions and thinker of our thoughts, since there is no "you" and "I" to be a doer or a thinker. Thoughts and actions happen as naturally as the wind blows and the rain falls. This may seem to be a doctrine of passive fatalism which pictures us as nothing more than puppets of predestined fortune. But this is to miss the deeper teachings. Actually there are no separate individuals to be controlled by anything. There is only the flow of Tao.

MARCH

The Wise know there is no one to go anywhere.
There is seeing but no one looking.
Doing naturally arises from Being.

LAO TZU

MARCH

All beings are parts of the Whole.
Their actions don't come from their own free will,
but as expressions of its laws.

CHUANG TZU

MARCH

Nature and destiny can not be altered.
Time can not be stopped.
Evolution can not be obstructed.

LAO TZU

MARCH

You don't make anything happen.
Events happen by themselves.

LAO TZU

MARCH

A one-legged dragon called Hui asked a centipede, "How do you manage all those legs? I can hardly manage one!" The centipede replied, "As a matter of fact, I don't manage my legs. They manage themselves."

MARCH

The Wise know they have no name.
They understand they have no self.
They realize they perform no acts.
They are one with Oneness.

CHUANG TZU

MARCH

Shun asked Cheng, *"Can you come to possess Tao?"* Cheng answered, *"You don't even possess your own body, yet you aspire to possess Tao!"* *"If my body is not mine, whose is it?"* asked Shun. Cheng replied, *"Your body is on loan from Heaven and Earth for a short time. Your every activity is an integral part of the great flux. You are pushed forward in life by you know not what. You don't even know how you assimilate the food that nourishes you. How can you call anything your own?"*

MARCH

Those who believe in fate no longer believe that, through their own efforts, they can prolong their life, succeed in their endeavors, or avoid misfortune.

THE YELLOW EMPEROR

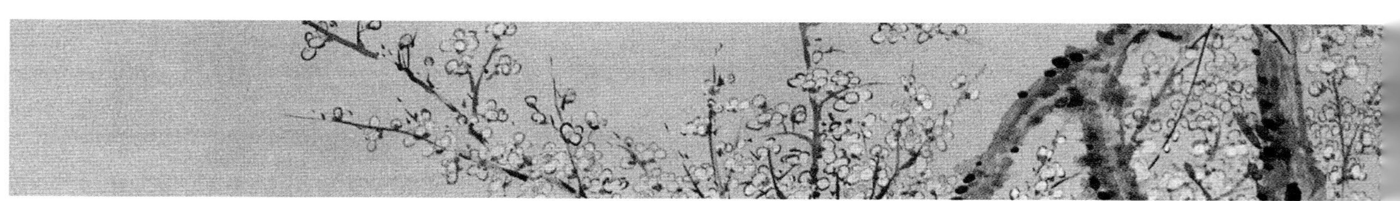

道牛

MARCH

Effort and Destiny were arguing about who is the most powerful. Destiny let fly an unending barrage of evidence to prove his superiority, concluding: "My dear Effort, if you are so effective why don't you make hardworking people rich and give good people a long life? And why are the intelligent unemployed and fools occupying important roles in government?" Embarrassed, Effort admitted: "You are right. Even when I seem to act, it is actually you who is acting."

MARCH

The enlightened are like living corpses.
They move because they are moved.
They don't think about their actions.
They aren't preoccupied with opinions.
No one can upset them.
They simply follow their fate.

YANG ZHU

MARCH

All beings form a ceaselessly transforming Whole. Therefore, the Wise don't praise or blame this person or that person, but give all their praise to the cosmic Oneness.

THE YELLOW EMPEROR

MARCH

The enlightened no longer rail against Heaven.
They don't resent other people.
They aren't filled with anxieties about business.
They aren't consumed with fear of the supernatural.
They know that their actions are Heaven's actions.
Their rest is the Earth's repose.

CHUANG TZU

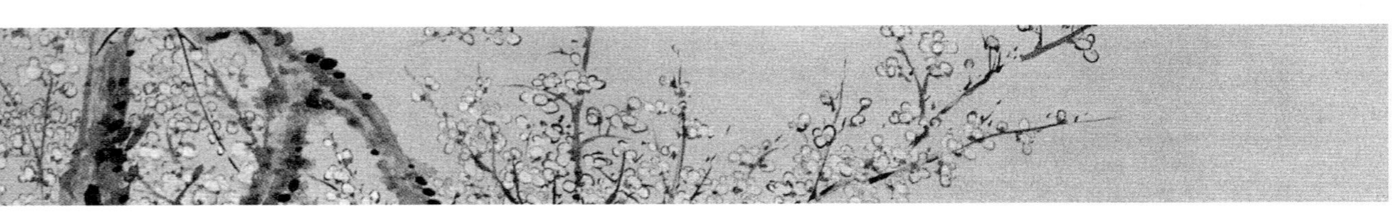

MARCH

Four desires disturb our peace: The desires for a long life, fame, social prestige, and wealth. Those without these things are given no rest by their dissatisfaction, and those with these things live in constant fear of losing them. It is the opposite with those who entrust their lives to destiny. They are not worried about these things. They are always satisfied and at peace because they have understood that everything is preordained.

YANG ZHU

MARCH

If you want what fate wants,
then nothing can happen against your will.

CHUANG TZU

MARCH

Tao brings each individual nature
back into harmony with the universal Nature,
each particular being into alignment
with the primordial Being,
the great Void, the supreme Whole.
This return is not achieved through doing something,
but through being a non-doer.
This doctrine of silent union seems foolish to fools,
but is actually mystical enlightenment,
through which one dissolves into the evolving cosmos.

CHUANG TZU

道牛

MARCH

To actively seek union with Tao is
to attempt the impossible.

CHUANG TZU

MARCH

Before acting, one should rest in a state of equanimity,
indifferent to the results of the action,
so that the action happens naturally
without any sense of it being "your" action.

CHUANG TZU

MARCH

Don't try to be a non-doer.
This is artificial and contrived.
Becoming a non-doer
isn't something you can do.

LAO TZU

MARCH

When everything is working naturally,
the eye sees, the ear hears, the nose smells,
the mouth tastes, the mind perceives,
and the heart spontaneously responds
with the appropriate action.

CHUANG TZU

MARCH

The Wise don't regard themselves
as doers or non-doers,
as alive or dead.
They are merely borne along
by the current of universal evolution.

CHUANG TZU

DEATH

For the Taoist sages, death is not the end. It is just another change of form in the perpetually transforming Tao. Death and life are two sides of the one reality. They are another expression of the polarity of Yin and Yang. Without death there could be no life. Without life there would be no death. They are parts of the one organic process through which Tao appears to evolve and transmutate. Death is the natural culmination of life which inevitably comes when it must. Life and death are extreme manifestations of the everyday dialectic between continuity and change, which creates us afresh and the same in every moment. We are constantly being born to the future and dying to the past, yet we remain what we are. What is there to fear?

道牛

MARCH

One should not consider death as a tragedy. Annihilation is not total. True, the physical self ceases to exist. But the impersonal transcendent Self continues.

CONFUCIUS

MARCH

There is a chain of transformation through which the Self persists. I am happy to be in a human body for this time, as I have been in the past and will be again in the future. I am content to be in a limitless succession of different forms. Why then should I fear death? It is the beginning of my next period of contentment.

CHUANG TZU

MARCH

Duke Jing was returning home after a long journey when he caught sight of his capital city in the distance. He was deeply moved and began to cry, saying, *"Oh beautiful city, why must the time come when I will leave you for good? If only human beings did not have to die!"* Two of the Duke's companions began to weep also, to please their master, saying, *"If the thought of death is painful to us mere servants, how terrible it must be to you, a great Duke."* Hearing all this, Yen Tzu, who was traveling with the party, burst out laughing. The duke was astonished. *"Why are you laughing while we all weep?"* he asked. Yen Tzu replied, *"If as you wish men did not die, all the great Dukes who have been your ancestors would still be alive and you would be a minor official far from the throne. You owe all your privileges to death. In regretting death you are being most ungrateful to all of those who have done you the great service of dying."*

道牛

MARCH

How do I know that when I die here I will not be born somewhere else?

LIN LEI

MARCH

Why should we not assume that life and death are equally good?

LIN LEI

MARCH

Perhaps we should look upon life as a swelling tumor or a protruding goiter, and upon death as the draining of a sore or the bursting of a boil.

CHUANG TZU

MARCH

When Lieh Tzu was wandering with his companions he came upon a skull, and, picking it up, announced, "He and I know that the difference between life and death is only imaginary. He through experience and I through understanding. We both know that clinging to life and fearing death is crazy, because they are two successive phases of the same process."

道牛

APRIL

Life terminates in a sleep
that is followed
by a new awakening.

CHUANG TZU

APRIL

The ancients knew that life is only a temporary visit to this world, and death is only a temporary withdrawal.

LIEH TZU

APRIL

A being dies over and over again. It receives a particular form for the duration of a particular existence, which is equivalent to the active period of daytime. Then it dies, which is equivalent to resting at night. And so it continues through the chain of time. What sort of new being it becomes depends on its spiritual merit, but it doesn't comprehend this process which it experiences as the hand of fate.

CONFUCIUS

APRIL

Death is to life what returning is to going away.
Death is a return to where we set out from when we were born.

LIN LEI

道牛

APRIL

Life is the cause of death.

YEN CHENG TZU

APRIL

Existence and nonexistence
are the undulating pulse of Tao.

LAO TZU

APRIL

That life and death could be aspects of each other seems unbelievable to most people. Will this ever change? I doubt it!

CHUANG TZU

APRIL

Chuang Tzu's wife died. When Hui Tzu went to convey his condolences, he found Chuang Tzu sitting with his legs sprawled out, pounding on a tub and singing. "You lived with her. She brought up your children. You grew old together," said Hui Tzu. "It is amazing that you are not weeping at her death. To be pounding on a tub and singing – this is going too far!"

Chuang Tzu said, "You're wrong. When she first died, do you think I didn't grieve like anyone else? But I looked back to her beginning. Before she was born. Before she had a body. Not only the time before she had a body, but the time before she had a spirit. In the midst of the jumble of wonder and mystery a change took place and she had a spirit. Another change and she had a body. Another change and she was born. Now there's been another change and she's dead. It's just like the progression of the four seasons – spring, summer, fall, winter. Now she's going to rest peacefully in vast empty space. If I were to follow after her, bawling and sobbing, it would show that I don't understand anything about fate. So I stopped."

道
牛

APRIL

Qin Shi went to mourn the death of his friend Lao Tzu. When he came out from seeing the coffin his followers asked him, "You were a friend of Lao Tzu. Why did you not weep?" Qin Shi replied, "This body is no longer my friend. All these mourners filling the house with their horrendous howling are just being sentimental and unreasonable. The sage remembers the law of life: that each one of us comes into the world and leaves it at the appointed time."

APRIL

You haven't been able to prevent your birth
and you won't be able to prevent your death.

CHUANG TZU

APRIL

Being worried does not lengthen life
and lack of care does not shorten it.
Caring for the body does not improve it
and disregarding it does not weaken it.
Sometimes indeed the opposite seems to be true.
One lives or dies because one should.
One cannot change fate one way or the other.

LIEH TZU

APRIL

The alternation of life and death
is as predetermined by Heaven
as is the rotation of day and night.

CHUANG TZU

APRIL

The Wise consider a thousand human lives as part of one process of evolution. They experience ten thousand differences as aspects of one Source.

LAO TZU

APRIL

When beings return to formlessness at death,
they retain reality without place
and duration without time.
This is the nature of Tao – the cosmic Oneness.

CHUANG TZU

APRIL

At the moment of dissipation, if your spirit is strong, you may escape the influence of Heaven and Earth and merge with the great Whole.

CHUANG TZU

APRIL

All beings ceaselessly change their form.
The giver of these forms is unknown.
The rule he follows is mysterious.
What can anyone know about their end?
There is nothing for it
but to wait patiently and see what will happen.

CONFUCIUS

THE NATURAL WAY

Taoism is not just about abstract metaphysics. It offers practical guidance to help us awaken to Tao. Taoism is the way back to the Way. It is sometimes called "The Natural Way" because it teaches us to return to our innate instincts. It urges us to free ourselves from the arbitrary cultural prejudices that we have inherited from those around us and glimpse our own essential nature. It encourages us to be what we are, not what we have been taught we should be. It is by uncovering our own genuine nature and expressing it authentically that we become aware of the universal Nature which is Tao.

道
牛

17
APRIL

At the foundation of everything is Nature.

CHUANG TZU

18
APRIL

Confucius taught that we must sing according to certain scales and live according to certain laws and decide moral questions according to what others say and submit completely to the customs of the state whatever they may be, and so on and on and on. Stop! Enough! I cannot go along with this nonsense. To live well we need only follow our natural instincts.

CHUANG TZU

道牛

APRIL

Social conventions lead you away
from the natural way of things.

LIEH TZU

APRIL

The Wise are not bound by the norms of society. Those who are caught up in cultural customs are inevitably constrained physically and drained mentally. This is the price of allowing themselves to be directed from the outside.

LAO TZU

APRIL

Why not live your own life,
not the life that others say you should?

LIEH TZU

APRIL

When Confucius finally understood the errors of his ways and embraced Taoism, he sent his followers away and hid himself among the reeds of a swamp. He dressed in animal skins and lived on acorns and chestnuts. Eventually he returned to such a state of natural living that his presence no longer frightened the birds and beasts. Even people began to find him quite bearable.

CHUANG TZU

APRIL

When Chuang Tzu was dying, his disciples planned to collect money among themselves to give him an honorable funeral. Chuang Tzu, however, announced: *"I don't want any of that ritual nonsense. I will have Heaven and Earth as my coffin and the jewels that adorn it will be the sun, the moon, and the stars, and the whole of Nature will be my burial procession. Could you buy me anything better than this?"* His disciples insisted, saying, *"We will not leave your body unburied to be eaten by vultures and crows."* Chuang Tzu laughed and replied. *"So instead you would bury it to be eaten by ants and worms. Delivered from birds to be devoured underground by insects!"*

道牛

APRIL

A corpse is like an old cast-off coat.
What difference does it make if you burn it,
bury it,
throw it in a river,
cover it with riches,
tie it up with straw?
It all comes to the same thing.

GUAN ZHONG

APRIL

Stop worrying and being always busy and you will conserve the life force that protects the body. If your body and spirit are strong and healthy, you will be unified with Nature.

CHUANG TZU

APRIL

If you try to defy Nature you will suffer the consequences.

LIEH TZU

APRIL

One should not do violence to the way things naturally are, even from the desire to improve them. See that you don't try to lengthen a duck's feet or shorten a crane's legs. This would only cause them suffering, which is the characteristic of everything that is against Nature.

CHUANG TZU

APRIL

Hui Tzu said to Chuang Tzu, *"This old tree is so crooked and rough that it is useless for lumber. In the same way, your teachings have no practical use."*

Chuang Tzu replied, *"This tree may be useless as lumber, but you could rest in the gentle shade of its big branches or admire its rustic character. It only seems useless to you because you want to turn it into something else and don't know how to appreciate it for what it is. My teachings are like that."*

APRIL

Attraction, the King of the Southern Sea, and Repulsion, the King of the Northern Sea, were friendly with Chaos, the King of the Center. One day they decided they would do something to help their friend. They observed that human beings have seven orifices – two eyes, two ears, two nostrils and a mouth – while Chaos didn't have any at all. So they decided to make him some. They made one orifice a day until on the seventh day Chaos had seven orifices. He therefore ceased to be chaotic, and so, to Attraction's and Repulsion's dismay, Chaos inevitably died!

CHUANG TZU

APRIL

All beings should be left in their natural deprived state. One should not attempt to perfect them artificially. Otherwise they cease to be what they are and what they should remain.

CHUANG TZU

道牛

MAY

All things have their unique place in the universe. They fulfil their roles simply by being what they are.

LIEH TZU

MAY

Different writers have suggested various ways to govern the world, each regarding his own solution as the best. As it turns out, however, they are all useless. There is only one way which works – allowing Tao to perform its magic naturally without hindering it.

CHUANG TZU

MAY

From ancient times people have followed diverse desires, rather than their true natures. Common folk kill themselves for money, the educated for reputation, the nobility for glory, and politicians for the empire. All these different types have this in common – they all act against Nature and are thereby ruined. What does the diversity matter if the results are the same?

CHUANG TZU

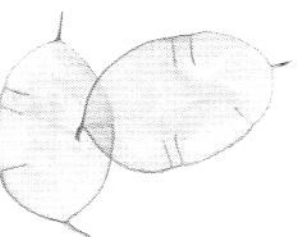

道牛

MAY

Every human being's essential nature is perfect and faultless, but after years of immersion in the world we easily forget our roots and take on a counterfeit nature.

LAO TZU

MAY

Anything artificial is false and ineffective.
Only what is natural is true and effective.

CONFUCIUS

MAY

Those who imitate others deform their own natures. Whether they be regarded as "bandits" or "sages" doesn't matter to me. From my point of view, they have all gone astray, because the only rule is conformity or nonconformity to one's intrinsic nature.

CHUANG TZU

MAY

To be free from all constraints
and able to satisfy one's instincts day and
night – that's what I call living!

GUAN ZHONG

MAY

Living a life without any limits
is the highest state of existence.

LIEH TZU

MAY

The ear wants to hear music.
The eye wants to see beauty.
The nose craves fragrance.
The mouth desires to speak of what is true and false.
The body desires warmth and good food.
The mind wants to be at liberty to go where it wills.
If these natural urges are thwarted,
our very nature is repressed.
Tyrants suppress us in these ways.
Let us depose them and wait happily for death.

LIEH TZU

道牛

MAY

To follow one's natural appetites
is making good use of taste.
To listen to one's inner voice
makes good use of hearing.
To examine oneself
makes good use of sight.

CHUANG TZU

MAY

Those who are called "sages" are just people
who live according to their situation.
They eat according to the size of their bellies
and dress according to the size of their bodies.

LAO TZU

MAY

Zi Chan was Prime Minister. However, his brother Chao was a drunkard and his brother Mu was renown for his debaucheries. Zi Chan expressed his worries to Minister Deng Xi that people would think badly of him because he could not reform his wayward brothers. Deng Xi recommended that he try and impress on them the importance of proper standards of behavior. Zi Chan, therefore, lectured his brothers on the fact that it was polite manners, traditional rites, and religious rituals that made humans greater than mere animals. He assured them that if they satiated their passions they would ruin their reputations. Then finally he promised them positions at court if they changed their ways. Chao and Mu replied: "*We have heard all this before and decided it was a lot of nonsense years ago. Death comes soon enough. In our opinion, what matters is appreciating life. We aren't interested in making life a living death through pompous rites and rituals. To satiate one's instincts and exhaust oneself in every pleasure – that's really living! Our only regret is that our bellies are too small for our appetites and our bodies too weak for our lust. Why should we care what others say? We see things differently to you. You lay down rules concerning how to act and make men suffer through limiting their natural instincts. We believe letting one's instincts run free is the root to happiness. You may succeed in imposing your system on the state. But despite this, our way will always spontaneously arise within princes and paupers alike. So, thank you for explaining your opinions to us. We are glad to have been able to explain ours to you.*" Zi Chan was dumbstruck and returned to Deng Xi to tell him what had happened. Deng Xi only commented, "*You obviously didn't realize that your brothers see things more clearly than you do.*"

NATURAL GOODNESS

Tao expresses itself through its "Te." Te is the Natural Goodness of Tao, which creates and nurtures all beings. For the Taoist sages, therefore, goodness is not something that can be defined by any manmade moral code. It is not an ethical idea to be debated by philosophers. It is the essential nature of the universe. Goodness is naturally innate in each one of us. We will not become good, therefore, by forcing ourselves to fit a mold created by professional moralizers, but by living naturally. As long as we try to live up to an idea of what we should be, we will always fail and feel inadequate. However, if we can simply be what we are, we will live a good life, free from the unnecessary burden of artificial moral strictures.

道
牛

13
MAY

The Natural Goodness of Tao
presides over the process of cosmic evolution.

TAI GONG DIAO

14
MAY

There is a natural sense of right and wrong,
which vibrates in unison with Tao,
at the heart of every man and woman.

CHUANG TZU

15
MAY

Natural Goodness is obscured by self-interest.

LAO TZU

16
MAY

Morality made by the mind gets in
the way of Natural Goodness.

CHUANG TZU

17
MAY

When Tao is lost,
there is still Natural Goodness.
When Natural Goodness is lost,
there is still kindness.
When kindness is lost,
there is still justice.
When justice is lost,
there are only social niceties,
and these are not genuine or honest.
Then all is lost.

LAO TZU

道牛

MAY

There is no absolute right and wrong. People judge as right what they personally consider pleasant, and judge as wrong what they personally consider unpleasant. Convincing others of what is right cannot be equated with teaching the Truth. It is just teaching others to agree with you. It is not about putting an end to error, but putting an end to opinions contrary to your own preconceptions.

LAO TZU

MAY

The rich forbid theft and murder, and threaten offenders with the death penalty. Yet these same people encourage theft and murder by honoring wealth and status, which are the allurements of crime. As long as distinctions in ownership remain, can there ever be an end to conflict between people? Once rulers were grateful to their subjects during times of order, and during chaotic times looked for the fault in their own conduct. These days it's the complete opposite. The people are driven to lose their natural honesty and commit crimes. But who should take responsibility? The unfortunates who are punished, or the rich and powerful who provoke the crimes in the first place?

BO JU

MAY

If some poor devil steals a belt buckle, he is decapitated. If a powerful politician takes possession of a whole country, the professional moralizers flock to him to put their "wisdom" at his disposal. The logical conclusion is that, rather than wasting one's time with small thefts, one should steal a whole country. Then one will not have to go to the trouble of further thefts or have to fear the executioner's ax.

CHUANG TZU

MAY

Life rushes onward like a galloping horse, changing in every instant, and you ask me what one should and shouldn't do! Respond to the constantly changing circumstances in the immediacy of the moment. What else can you do?

CHUANG TZU

MAY

Similar actions in different situations do not produce the same results. One should adapt to the needs of the time.

LIEH TZU

23

MAY

Halfway may seem like a point of balance and therefore a good place to be. But is halfway between good and worthless really where you want to be? Better to drift with the currents of Tao. To be now a dragon, now a snake. Now up, now down. Shifting with the time and never willing to be tied down to one road.

CHUANG TZU

道牛

MAY

Tao follows no fixed rules.

HUAI NUN TZU

MAY

The Wise don't obey useless laws.

LAO TZU

MAY

Laws are written to bring about justice. To stick to the letter of a law so meticulously that it creates injustice is to take care of your hat and shoes while forgetting the head and feet they were designed to protect.

LAO TZU

MAY

Those who understand the spirit of a law adapt it to the changing times. Those who do not understand this continue to follow it even when to do so has become harmful.

LAO TZU

MAY

Decadence began with the introduction of the laws of marriage and family, which seemed like progress but which actually inaugurated the ruin of the primordial simplicity and promiscuity.

CHUANG TZU

MAY

A man's son ran away from home, so the man had a drum beaten loudly to signal that there was to be a search party sent forth. The son, however, hearing the sound, ran so far away that he was never seen again. Trying to reintroduce goodness into the world by moral coercion will have the same negative results, I fear. It will cause what is left of people's natural sense of right and wrong to flee even further away.

LAO TZU

MAY

The hardest heart may be softened by gentleness, but try to cut and polish it and it will burn like fire or freeze like ice.

LAO TZU

MAY

All official pronouncements designed to lecture people about what is morally good and just are artificial and against Nature.

CHUANG TZU

道牛

JUNE

I will not praise those who do violence to their nature by piously practicing phoney manmade morality. Human beings do not become good through practicing artificial goodness, but through living naturally.

CHUANG TZU

JUNE

A branch is cut from a living tree, then chiseled and painted to make a ritual vase. The leftovers are thrown away as rubbish. Everyone says that the vase is beautiful while the leftovers are ugly. I say both the vase and the leftovers are ugly, because they are no longer the natural, living tree. In the same way I judge virtuous saints and vicious sinners as equally misguided. Whether through good or bad motivation, both have acted against their true nature. Neither are natural human beings.

CHUANG TZU

JUNE

To die doing good for the love of glory and to die being executed for a crime come to the same thing.

CHUANG TZU

JUNE

Artificial goodness and justice are as odious to me as vice and depravity.

CHUANG TZU

JUNE

Abandon trying to seem good,
throw out self-righteousness,
and rediscover natural compassion.

LAO TZU

JUNE

Those who do good because they want to be seen to be good are not good.

LIEH TZU

JUNE

Give up trying to seem holy,
forget trying to appear wise,
and it will be a lot better for everyone.

LAO TZU

JUNE

The foot does not feel a perfect shoe.
The waist is not aware of a perfect belt.
The perfect heart is not concerned
with artificial ideas of good and bad.
It naturally acts well
and naturally abstains from evil.
Perfection is being perfect without knowing it.

CHUANG TZU

JUNE

An orchid doesn't lose its fragrance
just because no one notices how good it smells.
A boat doesn't sink
just because no one notices how sturdy it is.
The Wise don't abandon Tao
just because no one notices how wise they are.
It is their nature to be the way they are.

LAO TZU

JUNE

To be perfectly pure,
accept appearing not to be.

LAO TZU

JUNE

In the whole of history there has never existed a single person whose conduct was always perfect. Understanding this, the Wise don't try to be perfect.

LAO TZU

JUNE

If you focus on people's foibles and not their qualities, you will find it difficult to find a single good person in the whole world. There is no one who does not have shortcomings. It is the human condition.

LAO TZU

JUNE

There is no one who is either valuable or worthless. If you value someone for what is valuable about them, everyone is valuable. If you regard someone as worthless for what is worthless about them, everyone is worthless.

LAO TZU

AWAKENING

The enlightened sages compare our ordinary consciousness to a dream. Reality is found when we wake up. This is a gradual process of expanding our awareness. It is an evolution which is the essence of the life process. It is not achieved by doing anything, but rather by ceasing to agitate the mind with restless thoughts, so that it settles down into a state of primal simplicity. When we do this, enlightenment spontaneously happens. We see through the veil of transitory appearances and find ourselves in silent communion with Tao.

14 JUNE

Fools regard themselves as already awake.

CHUANG TZU

15 JUNE

Love of life is an illusion, and fear of death is a mistake. Is life anything but a dream? Some who wake from a good dream are upset, while others who wake from a bad dream are pleased. Death is the great awakening, after which one says of life that it was a long dream. But few among the living understand this. Most believe themselves wide-awake! They actually believe they are kings and servants.

CHUANG TZU

16 JUNE

We're both dreaming – you and I.
I who tell you we are dreaming –
I am also just a part of the dream.

CHUANG TZU

17 JUNE

Everything we perceive as objectively true in this world is actually personal and subjective.

WANG NI

18

JUNE

I was a butterfly, flying contentedly.
Then I awoke as Chuang Tzu.
Now I don't know who I really am –
a butterfly who dreams he is Chuang Tzu
or Chuang Tzu who dreamed he was a butterfly.

CHUANG TZU

道牛

JUNE

Ordinary people don't think for themselves and believe that everything is real. But although blindness is ubiquitous, it is not universal. There are still those who have not been seduced by normal consciousness; who recognize no master but their own reason; who have, through meditation on the universe, come to understand that there is nothing real except Tao.

MASTER QI

JUNE

Waking thoughts and sleeping dreams are both equally illusionary. The Wise pay little attention to either.

LIEH TZU

JUNE

See the eternal beyond the impermanent.

LAO TZU

22

JUNE

If you are able to see through the illusion, you are in Heaven. If not, you find yourself in hell.

LIEH TZU

JUNE

Abandon small-mindedness
and you will avoid great delusions.
Expand your awareness
and you will decrease your foolishness.

LAO TZU

JUNE

A human body occupies only a little space,
but consciousness can reach to Heaven.

CHUANG TZU

道牛

JUNE

Yen Hui, a much-loved disciple of Confucius, said to his Master: *"Now I am really getting somewhere."* *"How do you know?"* asked Confucius. *"Because I have abandoned all concepts of goodness and justice,"* Yen Hui replied. *"Excellent. But there is farther to go,"* said Confucius.

JUNE

Yen Hui said to Confucius: *"Now I am really getting somewhere." "How do you know?"* asked Confucius. *"Because I have abandoned performing religious rites and rituals,"* Yen Hui replied. *"Excellent. But there is farther to go,"* said Confucius.

JUNE

Yen Hui said to Confucius: *"Now I am really getting somewhere." "How do you know?"* asked Confucius. *"Because when I sit in meditation I abandon absolutely everything."* Greatly moved, Confucius asked, *"What do you mean?"* Yen Hui replied: *"I cast off my body, still my mind, leave behind all forms, go beyond all knowledge, and unite myself with the One which penetrates all."* Confucius announced: *"This is that union in which all desires cease. It is the transformation in which individuality is subsumed. You have reached true wisdom. Please be my teacher from now on."*

道牛

JUNE

As the heart finds the changeless, it emits a natural light which illumines all within that is still phoney. With time, the artificial disappears and only the natural remains.

CHUANG TZU

JUNE

When I taught Liang Yu about Tao, after three days he became uninterested in the outside world. After seven more days he had abandoned the idea of there being objective things around him altogether. Nine days later he had abandoned the concept of his own independent existence. He then acquired that penetrating insight which reveals each moment as existing in an uninterrupted chain of Being. He understood that, in reality, killing doesn't cause death and begetting doesn't cause birth. Tao alone is the author of all endings and beginnings.

NU YU

JUNE

I have passed through various stages in my studies of Tao. After a year I rediscovered my natural simplicity. After three years I no longer had a sense of "you" and "me." After four years I was detached. After five years I began to live a good life. After six years my consciousness no longer wandered here and there but was entirely concentrated in my body. After seven years I entered communion with the universal Nature. After eight years I was no longer preoccupied with life and death. After nine years something mysterious happened and I found myself at one with Tao.

YEN CHENG TZU

道
牛

JULY

To merge with Tao,
turn away from your senses.
The light of pure Consciousness
hides in formlessness.

LAO TZU

JULY

Be empty. Be still.
Watch everything just come and go.
Emerging from the Source –
returning to the Source.
This is the way of Nature.

LAO TZU

JULY

It takes a whole day for a bowl of water to become still enough to reflect your face, but only one shake to make it so agitated that it reflects nothing. In the same way the human spirit is hard to clarify and easy to agitate.

LAO TZU

JULY

Our essential nature is happy, harmonious, clear, and serene. When you know your essence, you evolve spontaneously without doing violence to it.

LAO TZU

JULY

Be at peace.
Be aware of the Source.
This is the fulfillment of your destiny.
Know that which never changes.
This is enlightenment.

LAO TZU

JULY

Give up seeking all the time.
Perfection is to unite yourself silently
with the mysterious presence of Tao.

CONFUCIUS

JULY

Eventually you will experience the great awakening, and then you will discover that life is a great dream.

CHUANG TZU

KNOWING NOTHING

Tao is not discovered through learning, but through ignorance. Our opinions obscure our natural intuitive knowing. What we think we know is just that – a thought. Tao is what IS. We cannot know about Tao. We can only know Tao directly by being Tao. Struggling to achieve a rational understanding of reality is futile and will only exhaust us. Better to stop experiencing life via intellectual concepts, because it is only when the mind comes to a rest that we directly perceive the ever-present Mystery. Only when we fully acknowledge that we really do not know anything are we empty enough to be filled with Tao. Only when we understand that we can not possibly understand will we finally understand. Then we will know the nothing which is Tao.

JULY

The mass of people believe their judgments to be their own. They get very offended when it is suggested that they have actually received them ready-made from others and have simply been puppets of popular opinion all their lives. They speak in the current jargon and dress in the latest fashion – not from any personal sense of style but just to fit in. And these servile imitators actually believe they are self-determining. How ridiculous! This is an incurable sickness because people are convinced that they are not suffering from it. It is a universal madness, because everyone is infected. It is, therefore, a complete waste of time for me to try to return people to their own intrinsic instincts. Oh well!

CHUANG TZU

JULY

It is healthy to know you know nothing.
Pretending to know is a kind of sickness.
Realizing you are ill
is the beginning of healing.
The Wise are sick of sickness,
and so they are well.

LAO TZU

JULY

The Wise seem confused,
no matter how perfect their understanding.
They feel insufficient,
no matter how advanced they may be.

LAO TZU

JULY

Everyone knows that roosters go "cock-a-doodle-doo" and dogs go "bow-wow-wow," but not even the wisest can tell me why. It is the same with all of Nature. Make something so small that it becomes invisible or so big that it becomes incomprehensible – you will never extract its reason for being the way it is. How much less likely are you able to answer the greatest mystery of all – the "WHY?" of the universe.

TAI GONG DIAO

道
牛

JULY

Confucius met two boys who were arguing. One said: *"When the sun rises it is closer to the earth and at midday it is further away. I know this because it looks bigger when it rises in the morning and smaller at midday and distance makes objects seem smaller."* The other boy disagreed furiously, insisting: *"No. No. When it rises the sun is cool, but at midday it is hot. Therefore it must be nearer at midday because near things are warmer than distant things."* The two boys asked Confucius to settle their disagreement. Having thought for a while, Confucius had to admit, *"I don't know."*
"So why do they call you wise?" demanded the boys.
"Because I know that it is possible to prove anything with clever arguments," replied Confucius.

JULY

A man lost his ax and believed his neighbor's son had stolen it. The more he thought about it the more convinced he became, and every time he saw the boy his manner and expressions made his guilt beyond doubt. Then the man came across the ax when he cleared out his manure pit. When he met the boy again he appeared obviously to be the most honest young fellow anyone could hope to meet.

LIEH TZU

14

JULY

Be wary of making judgments, because even the ancient sages were ignorant of many things.

LIEH TZU

JULY

People mistakenly seek for the truth in books which necessarily only contain false ideas.

CHUANG TZU

JULY

The great classics are out of date.
They relate to circumstances
that no longer exist. What can you
deduce from an old footprint?

LAO TZU

JULY

Duke Huan was studying a book, when the wheelwright Pian asked him, *"What are you reading?"* The Duke replied: *"The words of the sages." "Living sages or dead sages?"* asked Pian. *"Dead sages; and what business is it of yours?"* replied the Duke, becoming irritated. Pian said, *"I was just considering that when I make a wheel it is easy to work the wood too softly or too strongly. But if I just do it instinctively, without thinking about it, I always create a beautiful wheel. I cannot tell you how I do it. It is a knack I am unable to teach my son so that, even now at the age of seventy, if I want a good wheel I have to make it myself. Were your dead sages any more able to write about their knack for living? If not, their books contain only the refuse left after the spirit has departed."*

JULY

The great leaders of antiquity took different roads to the same destination. They acted differently, with the same intention, depending on the circumstances. Intellectuals today, who have no knowledge of Tao, just pore over the footprints they left.

LAO TZU

道牛

JULY

Qu Bo Yu lived for sixty years, and in this time he changed his opinions sixty times. Fifty-nine times he was absolutely convinced he was right, and fifty-nine times he was forced to admit he was wrong. And who knows if his sixtieth opinion, which he held when he died, was any better than the rest? This happens to anyone who focuses on the details of things and has only a confused understanding of Tao.

CHUANG TZU

JULY

A man who had been born blind asked someone to describe the sun to him. This person said: *"It is like a brass tray."* The blind man struck a brass tray and heard a ring. Later when he heard a bell he thought, *"That's the sun."* Those who try to understand Tao without experiencing it directly themselves are often similarly misled.

SU TUNGP'O

JULY

Wishing to know too much is what wears you out.

GUANG CHENG

JULY

Prolonged and exaggerated mental effort uses up one's life force.

CHUANG TZU

JULY

Trying to understand is like straining to see through muddy water. Be still and allow the mud to settle.

LAO TZU

JULY

The true reason for things is indefinable and ungraspable. Only when returned to a state of primal simplicity through profound contemplation can consciousness partially see into these dark depths.

GUAN YIN TZU

JULY

Turn away from your senses,
forget your hopes and plans,
ignore the brilliance of your
intellect, and return to the unconscious
vastness of unknowing.

LAO TZU

JULY

What's the good of thinking about things?
Tao is the unconscious.
He who lives unconsciously
naturally follows his nature.
We are born spontaneously
without being asked
who or what we wish to be.
Nature wishes us likewise to
return to the Source
without having known
who we are or why we exist.

HONG MENG

JULY

Nothing is gained by thinking about Tao.
Tao is only known through silent contemplation.
To truly understand this is the beginning of enlightenment.

LAO TZU

JULY

To know Tao
it is necessary, above all,
to stop thinking.

THE YELLOW EMPEROR

JULY

The deepest form of devotion
is not to perform religious rites.
The best rule of conduct is to laugh at everything.
The most profound use of intelligence
is to think of nothing.

CHUANG TZU

JULY

Ran Qiu asked Confucius: *"Is it possible to know that which existed before Heaven and Earth?"* Confucius replied: *"Yes. It is that which is right here and now – eternal Tao."* Ran Qiu was profoundly inspired by these teachings, but returned to Confucius the next day and said, *"Yesterday I thought I understood your answer to my question, but today I am not sure I do. Please say more."* Confucius replied: *"Yesterday you used your natural intuition, which spontaneously swells up when the mind is empty, and so you immediately grasped what I was saying. Since then you have resorted to artificial logic, which has obscured the evidence of your immediate intuition. All I really said was 'that which was is that which is' – for there is no past or future, beginning or ending, in the ever-present mystery of Tao."*

JULY

All the ancient sages knew about knowledge
was that a simple sense of things,
which did not trouble them,
emanated spontaneously
from the calm of their inner nature.

CHUANG TZU

道牛

AUGUST

My body is intimately united with my mind, and both are intimately united with the cosmos, which is intimately united with the undefinable primal formlessness of Tao. Because of this intimate unity I know every harmony and discord that sounds in the universal symphony, but I cannot say how it is that I know.

GENG SANG TZU

AUGUST

Chuang Tzu and Hui Tzu were walking by a stream when Chuang Tzu remarked, *"Look how the fish are enjoying themselves, jumping out of the water."* Hui Tzu replied: *"You are not a fish; how could you know what they enjoy?" "You are not me,"* riposted Chuang Tzu, *"how could you know what I know and don't know. I know the fish are enjoying themselves just by observing the obvious."*

道牛

AUGUST

Preoccupied with the quest to learn what they do not naturally know, men lose the intuitive knowledge they already naturally possess.

CHUANG TZU

AUGUST

Someone seeking learning knows more and more.
Someone seeking Tao knows less and less –
until things just are what they are.

LAO TZU

AUGUST

Wisdom is knowing when to stop speaking, because language is inadequate.

CHUANG TZU

AUGUST

All theories are completely false.

CHUANG TZU

道牛

AUGUST

Why spend your life trying desperately
to understand this confusing existence?
It is better to understand
that the mind can understand nothing,
to accept willingly that there is no free will,
and then, without fear, to act or rest
according to the needs of the situation.

LIEH TZU

AUGUST

Fish traps exist to capture fish.
Once you've got the fish you can forget the trap.
Rabbit snares exist to capture rabbits.
Once you've got the rabbit you can forget the snare.
Words exist to capture meaning.
Once you've got the meaning, you can forget the words.
Where can I find a man who has forgotten words?
I'd like to have a word with him!

CHUANG TZU

GOING WITH THE FLOW

Taoism is often interpreted as a "quietist" philosophy that encourages us to do as little as possible. Certainly the ancient sages teach us to avoid doing anything unnecessary that interferes with the natural order of things, but they regard being wilfully inactive as just as artificial and unnatural as being too active. The Taoist sages are not concerned about how much we do or don't do. They want us to stop seeing ourselves as autonomous doers altogether and experience life as the unfolding of Tao. To come to this realization we must learn to let go and go with the flow. We must dare to willingly follow our fate. We must relinquish all the assumptions about what is good and bad that cause us to struggle against the current. We must finally abandon our futile fight to control our lives, and let life live us.

道牛

9

AUGUST

The Wise flow with Tao in life
and in death they merge
with the Oneness of things.

CHUANG TZU

10

AUGUST

Master Kui asked Nu Yu: *"How is it that, despite your great age, you still have the freshness of a little child?"* Nu Yu replied: *"Because I have lived my life in harmony with Tao and not worn myself out going against the flow of life."*

道牛

AUGUST

Be content with the moment
and be willing to follow the flow.

CHUANG TZU

AUGUST

Outwardly the enlightened seem the same as everybody else. Inwardly, however, their distinctive trait is that they have no goal, but simply allow life to unfold with no concern for where it is going. For them, effort, cunning, and purpose are the results of having forgotten one's true nature.

ZI GONG

AUGUST

Don't glorify the past and put down the present. No one can go against the current, so accommodate yourself to the nature of the times.

CHUANG TZU

AUGUST

Every time has its own nature, just as every being has its own nature – a nature that cannot be changed.

LAO TZU

AUGUST

Let everything go where it naturally wants to go and you will always be successful. Try to force things to go the way they don't want to go and you will have nothing but failure.

LAO TZU

AUGUST

Those who oppose the flow of Tao
end up being called "unlucky."

LAO TZU

道牛

AUGUST

Yen Xian was poor and Zi Gong was rich. Yen Xian worried about his poverty so much, he died. Zi Gong worried about his riches so much, he also died. If poverty and riches are equally harmful, what can one do? Just be happy with one's lot and neither can effect you.

YANG ZHU

AUGUST

The Wise focus their attention inside.
They understand calamity and fortune
as two aspects of the Oneness.

LAO TZU

AUGUST

You have no control over whether misfortune comes, but don't call it to you. You have no control over when good fortune comes, but don't reject it. When misfortune occurs, since you have not caused it, you will not experience grief. When good fortune comes, since you have not caused it, you will not glory in your achievement.

LAO TZU

AUGUST

Not even the best of smiths can melt wood.
Not even the best of carpenters can cut ice.
When nothing can be done about the way things are,
the Wise stop worrying about the situation.

LAO TZU

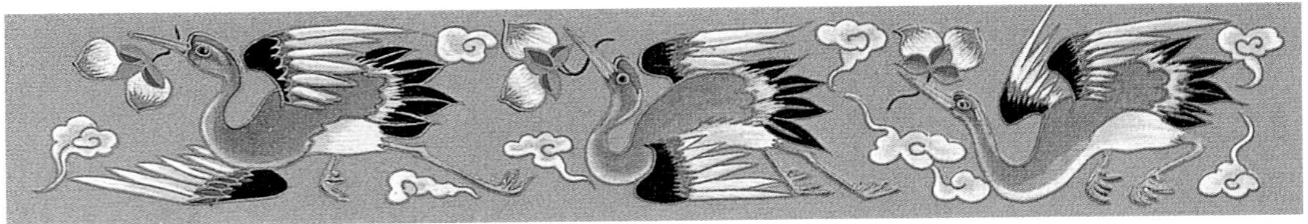

AUGUST

Ecstasy and anger.
Sadness and happiness.
Worry about the future and regret about the past.
Rashness and stubbornness.
Modesty and arrogance.
These are the mood music of the void.
Day and night, they follow one upon the other,
spontaneously emerging within us
from who knows where!
Let them be.
Moods are with us from morning until night.
We can't exist without them.
It is the way things are.
I don't know why.
If moods have a master,
then I have never met him.

CHUANG TZU

AUGUST

When I delight at the sight of the mountain forests or the high plains, sadness suddenly troubles my heart. Happiness and sadness come and go, regardless of my wishes. I cannot hold on to one and avoid the other. Must the human heart be a home to every momentary mood? Struggling to control them results in greater misery, because failure is certain when you attempt the impossible. There is only one viable option – to surrender to one's destiny, which comes from Tao.

CHUANG TZU

AUGUST

Mou was deeply unhappy about having been sent away from court to a seaside province. He expressed his sadness to Zhan Tzu, who told him *"Let go of these feelings or they may harm you." "I have tried and I just can't,"* explained Mou. *"In that case"*, said Zhan Tzu, *"give them full expression and weep, for to repress a powerful emotion is to inflict a double injury upon oneself. Those who do this do not live long."*

道牛

AUGUST

Once upon a time an old farmer lost his best stallion. His neighbor came around that evening to express his condolences, but the old farmer just said, "Who knows what is good and what is bad?" The next day the stallion returned, bringing with him three wild mares. The neighbor rushed round to celebrate, but the old farmer simply said, "Who knows what is good and what is bad?" The following day the farmer's son fell from one of the wild mares while trying to break her in, and injured his leg. The neighbor turned up to make sure that all was well, but the old farmer just said, "Who knows what is good and what is bad?" The next day the army came to conscript the farmer's son to go and fight in the wars, but finding him an invalid left him with his father. The neighbor thought to himself, "Who knows what is good and what is bad?"

道牛

AUGUST

What seems favorable can be fatal.
What seems fatal can be favorable.

LIEH TZU

AUGUST

The Wise are pleased by nothing
and pained by nothing,
delighted by nothing
and angered by nothing.
Everything is mysteriously the same.
There is no good and bad.

LAO TZU

AUGUST

Hardship, old age and death are regarded as the bane of human life, but the Wise accept them as necessary parts of the process of existence.

LIEH TZU

AUGUST

The acceptable and the unacceptable are both acceptable.

LAO TZU

AUGUST

For those at one with the Oneness, everything is good.

TAOIST SAYING

AUGUST

Nothing is wrong. Everything is right.

LAO TZU

AUGUST

Obtain as much joy from life as you can, and then accept death when it comes, for everything must end.

YANG ZHU

道牛

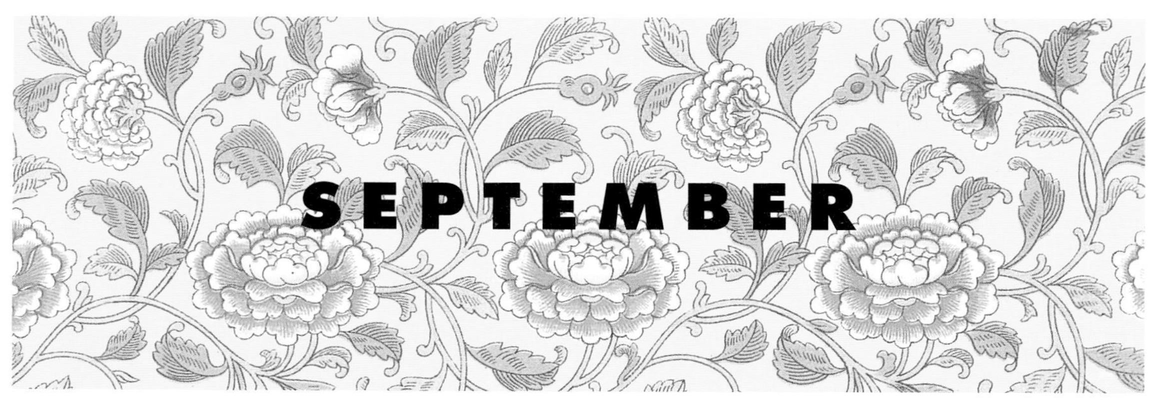

SEPTEMBER

Just surrender to the cycle of things.
Give yourselves to the wave of the Great Change.
Neither happy nor afraid.
And when it is time to go,
then simply go –
without any unnecessary fuss.

T'AO CH'IEN

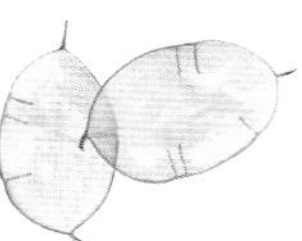

DETACHMENT

More than a thousand years after the time of Lao Tzu, the vibrant spirit of the ancient Taoist sages was rekindled by a new breed of Chinese masters, who synthesized Taoism with Indian Buddhism to produce Zen. One such sage, Seng-t'san, writes: "To follow Tao is easy for those that have no preferences." To be able to freely follow the flow of Tao requires us to relinquish our attachments to things being a certain way. We must be impervious to loss and gain, indifferent to praise and blame, unaffected by pleasure or pain. We must give up seeking wealth and fame, and accept whatever turns out to be our lot in life. We must allow our desires to naturally motivate our actions, just as, for example, thirst causes us to search for water. But we must not allow them to dominate us so much that we indulge ourselves in a fruitless attempt to control our uncontrollable lives. We must act, but without being attached to the results of our actions. We must do what we must do and then let go.

道牛

SEPTEMBER

If you want to be free,

forget about being comfortable.

If you want life,

avoid prestige.

If you want union with Tao,

let go of all your attachments.

CHUANG TZU

SEPTEMBER

Perfect virtue is compassionate detachment.

CONFUCIUS

SEPTEMBER

Be present but absent,
alive but dead.

LAO TZU

SEPTEMBER

Let go of the world
and return to the Self.

LAO TZU

SEPTEMBER

When people wager a piece of pottery they feel composed. When they wager money they become nervous. When they wager gold they completely lose their head. Their ability to function depends on freedom from distraction caused by attachment. Attachment to the outer troubles the interior.

CONFUCIUS

SEPTEMBER

A man had been born in the Kingdom of Yen but now lived in the Kingdom of Chu. As an old man he returned to the land of his birth. While on his journey his companions tricked him by saying of another town that it was his old home. Believing them, the old man became pale and nostalgic. They showed him a shrine and told him, *"This is your family shrine."* The old man began weeping. They showed him some graves and said, *"These are the graves of your ancestors."* The old man was completely overcome. Then his companions fell around laughing and told him it was a hoax, and that actually there was still some distance to travel until they would reach his old home. When the old man did finally see his own village, his family shrine and the graves of his ancestors, he felt so completely detached that he didn't experience any grief or nostalgia, and wondered why he had bothered to make such a long journey.

SEPTEMBER

The Wise enjoy nothing in particular,
and so enjoy everything in general.

LAO TZU

道牛

SEPTEMBER

The Wise live among people, but are indifferent to their praise or blame.

CHUANG TZU

SEPTEMBER

The man who has had his feet cut off in punishment discards his fancy clothes because praise and blame no longer touch him. The condemned convict climbs the highest peak without fear, because he has stopped worrying about avoiding death. You may treat such people with respect, but they will not be pleased. You may treat them with contempt, but they will not be angry. They don't care what others think about them. They are in harmony with Heaven.

CHUANG TZU

SEPTEMBER

Those who are one with the Oneness, who have lost an awareness of their own personality, who think of their body as dust, who consider life and death like day and night, for whom loss and gain are the same, who value social prestige as if it were mud – those who have this noble self-knowledge cannot be touched by the vicissitudes of life. They live in unison with Tao.

LAO TZU

SEPTEMBER

Dong Men Wu lost his son but did not grieve. His neighbor asked him, *"You clearly loved your son very much, why do you not weep?"* Dong Men Wu replied: *"Many years ago, before my son was born, I lived without him and was not sad. Why should I be sad now?"*

SEPTEMBER

Stick to being simple. Hold yourself in the Void.
Let go of everything. Desire nothing for yourself.
Then everything will follow its natural course.

WU MING REN

道牛

SEPTEMBER

If you desire emptiness this desire will fill up the emptiness. Just allow emptiness to spontaneously happen.

LAO TZU

SEPTEMBER

If we are not completely detached from the results of our actions, they inevitably result only in the undesirable.

CHUANG TZU

SEPTEMBER

If you indulge your desire to the extent that you lose touch with your essential nature, then everything you do is wrong.

LAO TZU

SEPTEMBER

Of all the weapons of death,
desire is the most murderous.

CHUANG TZU

道牛

18 SEPTEMBER

The essential nature of water is clear,
but mud pollutes it.
The essential nature of a human being is peaceful,
but desires pollute it.

LAO TZU

19 SEPTEMBER

Those who understand the nature of consciousness
see desires and fears as externals.

LAO TZU

20 SEPTEMBER

The Ancients said, *"Give up and you will succeed."* Is this empty nonsense? Try it. If you are sincere, you will find fulfillment.

LAO TZU

21 SEPTEMBER

The Wise succeed without intending to do so.

LAO TZU

道牛

SEPTEMBER

After enlightenment, one no longer wishes to have or to do anything. When you have seen the emptiness of all desires and actions, what could one wish for?

GUAN YIN TZU

SEPTEMBER

Don't worry and everything will naturally sort itself out.

LAO TZU

HUMILITY

Lao Tzu explains that the sea is the greatest body of water because it is lower than all streams and rivers. Paradoxically, greatness comes through humility – through selflessness, not self-aggrandisement. The glittering prizes of fame, wealth, and power seem to offer us fulfillment, but actually they are pernicious illusions that ultimately bring grief and confusion. We end up entrapped in an artificial world of intrigue, ego trips, and false values – forever cut off from our essential nature. By not seeking to put ourselves above others, however, we cease to identify with our separate identity and discover Tao – our shared essence. What greatness could be greater than this?

道牛

SEPTEMBER

Two important officials were sent by the King of Chu to offer Chuang Tzu the office of royal minister. They found the sage quietly fishing. Chuang Tzu listened to their offer and without looking up replied: *"I have heard that in his royal temple the King honors an ancient shell of a sacrificed turtle. Tell me, if someone had given the turtle the choice, do you think it would have preferred to die and have its shell so honored, or to have lived out its years dragging its old tail in the muddy swamp?"* *"It would have preferred to live,"* replied the officials. *"Tell the king that I too prefer to live in the muddy swamp, unhonored but free,"* concluded Chuang Tzu.

SEPTEMBER

Master Hui said to Chuang Tzu, *"Your teachings have great depth, but no one wants them because they have no practical value. They're like the Ailanthus tree whose wood is good for nothing."* Chuang Tzu replied: *"That suits me fine. Everything that has practical value soon perishes. The cunning marten is soon trapped for its fur. The strong yak is soon killed for its tail. The Ailanthus, on the other hand, grows on wasteland, spreading out as much as it likes, giving shade to wanderers and lay-abouts. It has no fear of the ax because, as you rightly say, it is good for nothing. Is it not good to be good for nothing?"*

SEPTEMBER

People believe they will find satisfaction in good food, expensive clothes, lively music, and exciting sex. But when they have all this they are still not satisfied. Having understood that happiness is not just about having one's material needs met, they desire prestige, fame, and recognition. Pulled by these glittering prizes and pushed by cultural pressure, people waste their short lives in pursuit of such goals. Their achievements may give them the illusion that they have gained something in their lives, but in reality they have lost a lot. They can no longer see, hear, feel, think, and act from their hearts. Social pressures from without dictate everything they do. They end up living the life others tell them to, not their own lives. Is this any different from being a slave or a prisoner?

LIEH TZU

SEPTEMBER

On the death of the great emperors Yao and Shun and the tyrants Jie and Zhou there remained only decaying corpses impossible to tell apart, giving off the same putrid smell. The good, the wise, the foolish, and the evil all die the same.

YANG ZHU

SEPTEMBER

Those who value their lives don't try to become famous.

CHUANG TZU

SEPTEMBER

People crave power, prestige, and wealth, but compared to having a human body these possessions are nothing.

LAO TZU

SEPTEMBER

If someone neglected his business to wander around aimlessly, people would say he was crazy. Yet those who completely ignore the inevitability of death and obsessively seek wealth and prestige are called sane!

YEN TZU

道牛

OCTOBER

It really doesn't matter if generations to come remember your name. You won't be there to see it.

LIEH TZU

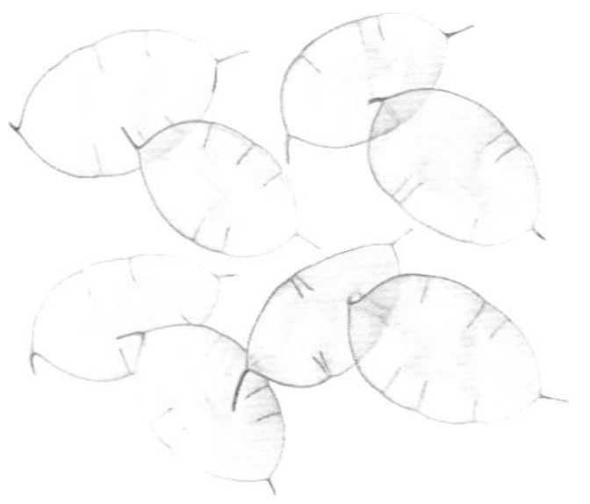

OCTOBER

You can't have it both ways. If you want integrity, then abandon trying to acquire status and wealth. If you want status and wealth, then you better accept that the price will be your integrity.

LIEH TZU

OCTOBER

The Wise shine without dazzling.

CHUANG TZU

道牛

OCTOBER

Although they may not intend to do so, those who do good to others acquire a good reputation. This in turn attracts good fortune. This inevitably makes enemies. Therefore the Wise question themselves many times before publicly doing good.

YANG ZHU

OCTOBER

Don't claim your achievements as your own and they will never be taken from you.

LAO TZU

OCTOBER

There is nothing so disastrous as admiring one's own achievements while depreciating the achievements of others.

CHUANG TZU

OCTOBER

Boasting dams the flow of good fortune.

GRAND DUKE REN

OCTOBER

Master Yang passed the night at an inn. The innkeeper had two wives. One very beautiful and one very ugly. The ugly wife was well loved, but the beautiful wife was not. Master Yang asked for an explanation. A young servant explained: *"The beautiful wife knows she is beautiful and flaunts it, so everyone deliberately ignores her beauty. Whereas the ugly wife knows she is ugly and effaces herself, so everyone deliberately ignores her ugliness."*

OCTOBER

If you understand how giving leads to receiving
and humility leads to glory,
you are close to understanding Tao.

LAO TZU

OCTOBER

Give up and you will succeed.
Bow and you will stand tall.
Be empty and you will be filled.
Let go of the old and let in the new.
Have little and there is room to receive more.

LAO TZU

OCTOBER

If you want to be valued,
first value others.
If you want to be respected,
first respect others.
If you want to overcome others,
first overcome yourself.
If you want to humble others,
first humble yourself.

LAO TZU

OCTOBER

All things appear as they truly are to those
who are not blinded by their own self-interest.
Their actions flow as naturally as water.
Their calm hearts reflect the truth without distortion.
They respond to a situation
like an echo responds to a sound.
They let go of self-interest and are aware of others.
They have no personal desires.
They don't want to be first,
but keep to always being the lowest.

GUAN YIN

道
牛

OCTOBER

The Wise stand out,
because they see themselves as part of the Whole.
They shine,
because they don't want to impress.
They achieve great things,
because they don't look for recognition.
Their wisdom is contained in what they are,
not their opinions.
They refuse to argue,
so no one argues with them.

LAO TZU

OCTOBER

The Ancient Masters understood Mystery.
The depth of their wisdom is unfathomable,
so all we have are descriptions of how they looked:
Careful as if crossing a frozen river,
alert as if aware of danger,
respectful like a guest,
yielding like melting ice,
simple like uncarved wood,
empty like a valley.

LAO TZU

OCTOBER

Leave gold in the depths of the rocks
and pearls in the depths of the sea.
Scorn wealth and fame.
Be indifferent to a long life and an early death.
Be neither vain when successful
or humiliated by failure.
Disdain possessions and avoid worldly glory.
Make your glory understanding
that all beings form a single universal complex,
and that life and death
are two aspects of the same existence.

CHUANG TZU

HARMONY

A life spent chasing the mirages of wealth, success, and fame is a wasted life. A life spent trying to force the world to change in accordance with our idea of what would be "better" is equally futile. One of these ways may seem selfish and the other altruistic, but to the Taoist sages both are unnatural and inauthentic. Fulfillment does not lie in these things, but in living in harmony with Tao. To do this our mind must become like calm water which perfectly reflects the way things are. Our reactions to life must be as instinctive and unaffected as an echo. This is the way we can benefit those around us. For only then will we truly have any peace and wisdom to offer a world enmeshed in illusion and suffering. The more we are in harmony with Tao, the more our world becomes in harmony with Tao.

道牛

OCTOBER

Happiness has nothing to do with wealth and prestige, but is a result of harmony.

LAO TZU

OCTOBER

The more you are in harmony with Tao the more perfect you will be.

CHUANG TZU

道牛

OCTOBER

A harmonious heart,
empty of self,
is the way to goodness.

LAO TZU

OCTOBER

Those whose minds rest in emptiness
perceive all beings as they are.
They are like a calm lake that reflects perfectly.
They are like an echo that repeats perfectly.
Unified with Tao they are in harmony with all beings.

GUAN YIN TZU

OCTOBER

Something too hard snaps.
Something too soft folds.
Too much kindness becomes weakness.
Too much discipline becomes harshness.
Too much love becomes indulgence.
Too much punishment becomes cruelty.
This is why harmony is best.

LAO TZU

OCTOBER

People have different natural characteristics. You cannot make a gregarious man live like a hermit or make a solitary man into a chatterbox. But all extremes, such as absolute solitude or continual company, are unnatural and to be avoided.

CHUANG TZU

OCTOBER

Those who are blind drunk may fall from a carriage and bruise themselves, but they won't die. Why not? Although their bones and joints are the same as anyone else's, at the moment of the fall their spirit is unconscious and so their hearts are not troubled by ideas of life and death, fear and hope. They do not tense. They don't resist the ground. So they don't break any bones. It is the same with those who live in harmony with Nature.

CHUANG TZU

OCTOBER

Everyone is attracted to someone
who lives in harmony with Tao,
because they are peaceful and happy.

LAO TZU

OCTOBER

No one looks for their reflection in running waters, but only in still waters. Likewise no one learns from a teacher with a restless mind, but only from the harmonious stillness of the true sage.

CONFUCIUS

OCTOBER

The Yellow Emperor had reigned over the empire for nineteen years, when he heard of Master Guang Cheng who lived on Mount Kong Tong. The Yellow Emperor sought him out and said, *"Master, I have heard that you are united with Tao. Please tell me its essence and I will use it to bring good crops to nourish my people. I will regulate the climate to benefit all living beings. Please teach me."* Master Guang Cheng replied *"You're ambitions are so great that you would even be the lord of Nature! To entrust the power of Tao to you would be a complete disaster for everyone. You would make it rain before the clouds had formed and make the leaves fall before they had become green. You conceited fool, what can you have in common with Tao?"* The Yellow Emperor returned home in confusion and spent three months in meditative retreat, living in a makeshift hut with a straw mat as the only furnishing. Eventually, he returned to Master Guang Cheng and begged on his knees, *"I know you are united with Tao, will you teach me how to likewise live in harmony?"* Master Guang Cheng replied: *"That is better. Come closer and I will teach you."*

OCTOBER

T'ien Ken was traveling to the south of Yin Mountain when he met a nameless sage. He respectfully requested, *"I beg you to tell me about how I may bring peace to the world." "Go away,"* muttered the nameless sage, *"You and your question are irritating me. I am enjoying the company of the Creator of all things. When I get tired I fly beyond the world on the bird of ease and emptiness, and wander in the land of nowhere, and live in the domain of nothingness. Why have you come to worry me with the problem of bringing peace to the world?"* T'ien Ken again respectfully asked his question and the nameless sage looked him deep in the eyes and replied: *"Set out to explore pure simplicity. Identify yourself with non-distinction. Follow the nature of things and don't let your personal prejudice distort your perception. For such a one the world is already at peace."*

道牛

OCTOBER

A man was afraid of his shadow and his footprints, so he started to run away from them. The more he ran, the more footprints he left. No matter how fast he ran, his shadow kept up with him. In desperation he ran faster and faster, until he dropped down dead. What a fool. If only he had sat in the shade he would not have produced a shadow. If only he had kept still, he would have produced no footprints. If only he had kept himself at peace, he would have had no problems.

CHUANG TZU

OCTOBER

To use this short finite life to grieve over the chaos of the world is like weeping into a river of tears for fear it will run dry. Only those who abandon worrying about the chaos of the world and create order in themselves can begin to understand Tao.

LAO TZU

OCTOBER

A traveler arrived at a remote village that was suffering from an extreme drought. In their desperation the villagers called in a Taoist sage, renowned for being a wonder-worker, to magically bring the rain. The rainmaker came to the village, looked around carefully and talked to the inhabitants. Then he built himself a little shack just outside the village and remained inside for three days and nights. After this time he emerged, took down his shack, and started to leave. As he did so, it began to rain. The visitor was amazed and ran after the departing sage. Catching up with him, he demanded: *"How did you bring the rain?"* The sage replied, *"Don't be silly. I didn't make it rain. I simply came to this village and saw that the inhabitants were out of harmony with Tao. This made me feel out of harmony with Tao, so I built myself a little shack and sat in contemplation until I had restored my harmony with the way things are. Having done that, I am now leaving." "So why has the drought ended?"* asked the traveler. The sage replied: *"When I am in harmony with Tao, everything around me comes into harmony with Tao. When there is harmony, the rains come naturally."*

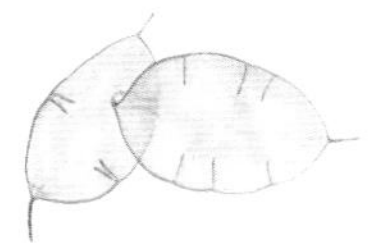

LOVE

Tao is unity. Love is an expression of its unifying power. Because they aren't full of themselves, the Taoist sages have space in their hearts for all beings. They understand that we are all manifestations of the one Universal Self and that being loving is not morally good or altruistic. It is simply the obvious thing to do. Compassion is a natural expression of our innate goodness. It is our greatest strength which can eventually overcome all obstacles just as soft water gradually wears away the hardest rocks. By treating the unkind with compassion, rather than bitterness and resentment, we put an end to the cycle of selfishness. We become a living testimony to the reality of Tao in which we are all kindred.

道
牛

30

OCTOBER

Embrace all beings,
for all are One.

CHUANG TZU

31

OCTOBER

Nurture your true nature.
Only talk the truth.
Make love your gift to others.

LAO TZU

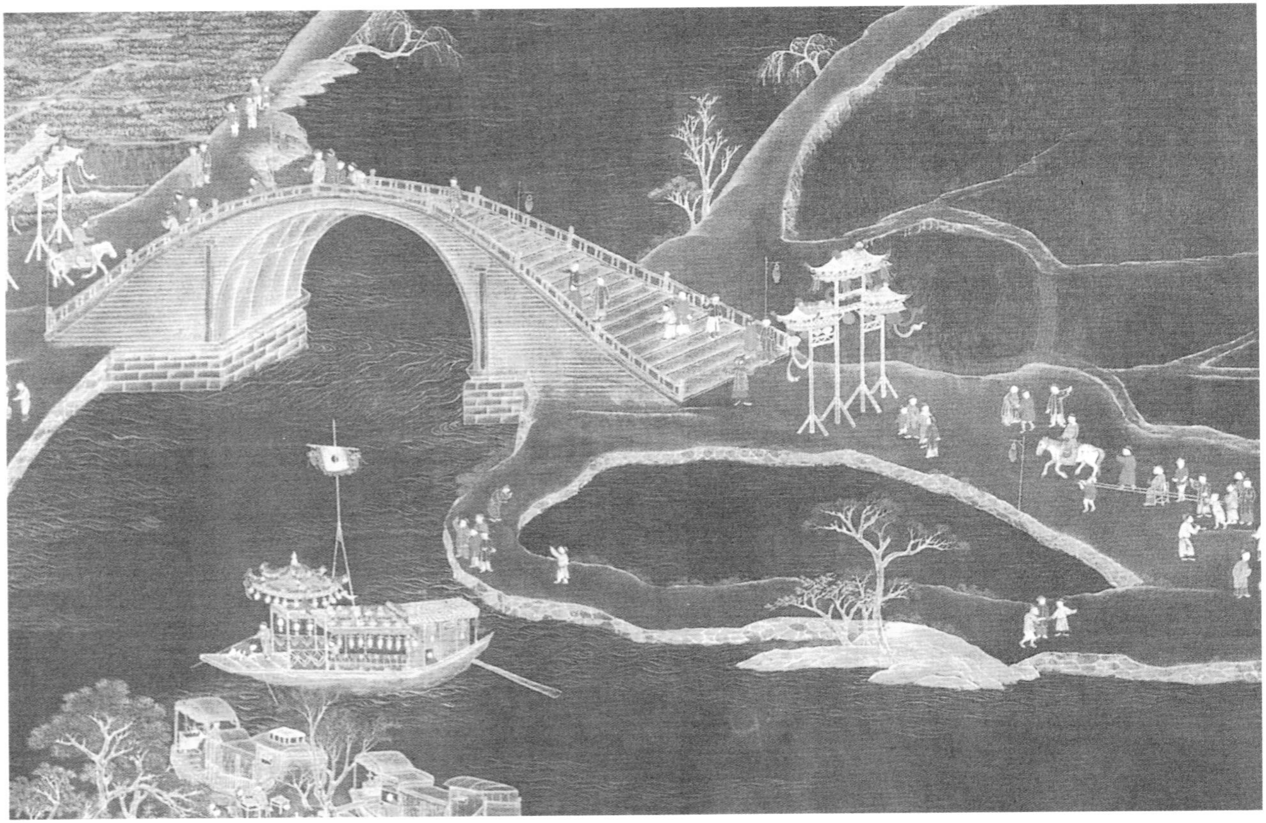

道牛

NOVEMBER

Make your heart like a lake
with a calm, still surface
and great depths of kindness.

LAO TZU

NOVEMBER

In conflict it is love that wins.
Love is the strongest protection.
If you have love,
it feels as if Heaven itself
is keeping you safe.

LAO TZU

NOVEMBER

Nothing wears away hard, strong rocks
as well as soft, weak water.
From this anyone can see that softness is harder than
hardness, and weakness is stronger than strength.
But no one lives accordingly.

LAO TZU

NOVEMBER

Softness and flexibility are the rulers of life.
Hardness and rigidity are the soldiers of death.

LAO TZU

NOVEMBER

The teeth may be harder than the tongue,
but they decay and fall out before the tongue does.

LAO TZU

NOVEMBER

When love accumulates it becomes good fortune.
When hate accumulates it becomes misfortune.

LAO TZU

NOVEMBER

If everyone's heart was full of love,
how could misfortune arise?

LAO TZU

NOVEMBER

If you can find no room in your heart for others
you will always feel like a stranger among strangers.

CHUANG TZU

道牛

9

NOVEMBER

The Wise lend themselves to others,
without giving themselves away.

CHUANG TZU

10

NOVEMBER

Through the simple art of gentle conversation the Wise charm away people's sufferings and help them accept their lives.

CHUANG TZU

11

NOVEMBER

Being a good listener
spares one the burden of giving advice.

LAO TZU

道牛

NOVEMBER

The Wise aren't full of themselves.
The more they do for others,
the more they feel fulfilled.
The more they give to others,
the more they feel they have.

LAO TZU

NOVEMBER

Day and night the Wise never forget
their desire to help others.

LAO TZU

NOVEMBER

I am good to the good and I am good
to the bad, because it is good to be good.
I trust the trustworthy and I trust the untrustworthy,
because I trust in trust.

LAO TZU

NOVEMBER

Overcome unkindness
with compassion.

LAO TZU

NOVEMBER

One sees them everywhere – businessmen hoisting themselves up on tiptoe, struggling desperately to succeed. They are overflowing with anxieties so there is no longer even any room for love of their fellow beings. They are, therefore, themselves unloved and regarded as being no longer human.

CHUANG TZU

NOVEMBER

Heaven and Earth each have their respective deficits that they compensate reciprocally. The Wise know they likewise have their deficits which lead them to look to others. All beings need each other.

LIEH TZU

NOVEMBER

After an attempt at reconciliation,
if bitterness still remains – what then?
Meet bitterness with kindness.

LAO TZU

NOVEMBER

To imitate the unconscious benevolence of Heaven and Earth through which everything spontaneously evolves, do good to all beings without anyone noticing.

CHUANG TZU

NOVEMBER

Buy captive animals and set them free.
Dispense with the butcher and abstain from death.
While walking be mindful of worms and ants.
Be careful with fire when in woods and forests.
Don't go to the mountain to trap birds in nets.
Don't travel to the river to poison fishes.
Don't slaughter the ox that ploughs your field.

TRACT OF THE QUIET WAY

NOVEMBER

Tain of Qi gave a great banquet for a thousand guests. On seeing all the different meats he announced piously, *"Look how well we are blessed by Heaven which makes all these different fish, birds, and animals for our consumption."* All the guests agreed, except a twelve-year-old boy who said, *"That's not true. It is a fact that the stronger and clever eat the weak and stupid, but don't conclude from this that one was made for the other to devour. Humans eat certain animals, but Heaven did not make them for this purpose. Otherwise we would have to also conclude that Heaven created humans in order that mosquitoes could feed on them."*

NOVEMBER

Prime Minister Tang asked Chuang Tzu, *"What is goodness?"* Chuang Tzu replied, *"Being like a tiger or a wolf." "What do you mean?"* asked Tang. *"Tigers and wolves care for their little ones and so should we,"* said Chuang Tzu. *"Yes. But what is Supreme Goodness?"* asked Tang. *"Supreme Goodness is not caring,"* replied Chuang Tzu. *"Then the man who is supremely good will not care for his family?"* asked Tang. *"No. That's not it,"* explained Chuang Tzu. *"Supreme goodness is not contrary to specific expressions of love, but it is a universal love which is wholly unconditional and undifferentiating. It is a love so high that the individual object of affection is lost to sight."*

道牛

道牛

NOVEMBER

When the streams dry up the fish huddle
together to try and keep themselves moist.
People admire this compassionate co-operation.
But would it not have been better if the fish
had earlier sought safety in deeper waters?

CHUANG TZU

NOVEMBER

If you have social status, don't be arrogant.
If you are socially insignificant, don't be ashamed.
If you are wealthy, don't be proud.
If you're poor, don't steal.
Always nurture unconditional love for all beings.
This is what it means to be truly human.

LAO TZU

NOVEMBER

To be benevolent to all beings is true goodness.
To dissolve all differences into unity is true greatness.
Not wishing to dominate others is true depth of spirit.
Possessing things without becoming anxious is true wealth.
Following the dictates of Heaven is the way to true success.
To be a willing vehicle of Tao is perfection.

CHUANG TZU

FOLLOWING THE WAY

Tao is the way to live in harmony with the way things are. It is not a way that can be pointed at by someone else, because it is not a fixed path to follow. It is a way that each one of us must discover for ourselves because it is a spontaneous expression of our own essential nature. All the Taoist sages can do is encourage us to listen to the inner voice of our own heart, to enjoy the moment, and to set out on a quest to rediscover our original simplicity. The irony, however, is that Tao is not a way from which we can ever deviate. It is reality. We are all flowing with Tao whether we know it or not. The difference between the Taoist sages and the rest of us is not that they are borne along by Tao while we are splashing about in fear of drowning; it is that we are so caught up in our ideas about life that we do not recognize the flow of Tao carrying us in every moment. Sometimes, usually when life seems good, we may say, "I really felt as if I was with the flow just then." But at other times we do not. When we relinquish the bothersome concepts of good and bad and fully enter into life we find that Tao is not a way we have to learn to follow. Tao is happening now and always will be. All there is and has ever been is Tao – eternally present, everchanging, and ever-the-same – the unspeakable Mystery.

NOVEMBER

Tao is not a way that can be pointed out.
A way that can be pointed out is not the Way.

LAO TZU

NOVEMBER

Tao is not something from which you can deviate.
A way that you can lose is not the Way.

THE DOCTRINE OF THE MEAN

NOVEMBER

Having high aspirations,
but without preconceived ideas;
working towards perfection,
but without following conventional moral codes;
governing impeccably,
but without attempting to become renown;
going within,
but not withdrawing from the world -
this is the way to follow Tao.

NOVEMBER

Following Tao is about living naturally,
not practicing spiritual gymnastics.

CHUANG TZU

NOVEMBER

If you stick rigidly to one spiritual discipline, even if you become a master of it, it is the same as blocking the flow of Tao by clinging to a small aspect of it.

LAO TZU

道牛

DECEMBER

Those who follow Tao do not make plans,
but act spontaneously
under the inspiration of the moment.
They completely disregard artificial notions
of right and wrong, good and evil.
They give to everyone alike,
just as one would give to lost orphans.
They satisfy all needs
without expecting anything back
or even hoping for thanks.
And they do all this
without ever being noticed.

ZHUN MANG

DECEMBER

The Wise are not burned by fire, drowned by water, frozen by cold, or harmed by ferocious beasts. Not because they posses magical powers which protect them, but because their circumspection helps them avoid these dangers.

CHUANG TZU

DECEMBER

The Wise don't blame
the sword that pierces them
or the brick that falls on them.
They seek the cause of their misfortunes
in their own imperfections.

CHUANG TZU

DECEMBER

A horse was tied up outside a shop in a narrow street and every time someone tried to walk down the lane it kicked out at the person. No one could work out what to do. Eventually someone called out, *"Look here comes Lao Tzu he'll know what to do."* Lao Tzu looked at the horse, considered the situation for a brief moment, turned around, and walked down another street.

DECEMBER

Flow around obstacles,
don't confront them.

LAO TZU

DECEMBER

Following the example of Tao,
the Wise meet all opposition
with a quiet mind and an open heart.
Then opposition naturally disappears.

LAO TZU

DECEMBER

The Wise transform the inner to make the outer enjoyable,
they don't try and transform the outer
to make the inner enjoyable.
They experience spontaneous enjoyment within themselves.

LAO TZU

DECEMBER

Ordinary people are friendly with those who are outwardly similar to them. The Wise are friendly with those who are inwardly similar to them.

LIEH TZU

DECEMBER

If I really believed that the mass of fools would listen to me, I would myself be a complete fool. Therefore, I leave them alone, without attempting to enlighten them. The truth is none of them are interested anyway!

CHUANG TZU

DECEMBER

Don't try and tell someone what you understand if they are incapable of understanding it.

BIAN TZU

DECEMBER

Some speak all their lives yet don't say anything. Others keep their mouths always shut yet say a lot.

CHUANG TZU

DECEMBER

Even if someone lives to be a hundred years old, a great part of that time is spent in the infirmities of childhood and old age. A huge part is consumed by sleep at night and worries by day. Much of it is wasted in sorrow and fear. Only a small fraction remains for enjoying being alive – so don't waste it.

YANG ZHU

DECEMBER

Don't waste time
calculating your chances
of success or failure.
Just fix your aim and begin.

GUAN YIN TZU

道
牛

道牛

14

DECEMBER

A thousand-mile journey starts with one step.

LAO TZU

15

DECEMBER

The secret of success is before attempting anything be very clear about why you are doing it.

GUAN YIN TZU

道牛

DECEMBER

Pick the right time and things will go well.
Miss the right time and things will go awry.

LIEH TZU

DECEMBER

The Wise do not value a huge gemstone as much as a little time. Time is hard to find and easy to lose.

LAO TZU

DECEMBER

When something enjoyable comes your way –
enjoy it completely!

LIEH TZU

DECEMBER

The Wise utterly devote themselves to everything in which they partake, every situation which contains them and within which they evolve.

CHUANG TZU

DECEMBER

The more creatively you live your life,
the more you will experience your essential nature.

LAO TZU

DECEMBER

The Wise witness events evolve,
yet keep to the Source.

LAO TZU

道牛

DECEMBER

Those who follow Tao don't seek to arrive anywhere,
so their journey is never over.

LAO TZU

DECEMBER

Following Tao in the world
is like being a mountain stream
that becomes part of a valley brook,
which becomes part of a great river,
which flows to the one sea.

LAO TZU

DECEMBER

We are not alive for very long, so we should not put off listening to the inner voice of our heart.

LIEH TZU

DECEMBER

The way to nurture life
is through abstract thoughts and happy feelings.

LAO TZU

DECEMBER

Tao is not far away from where you are.
Those who go looking for it elsewhere
always return to here and now.

LAO TZU

DECEMBER

Pick the right time and things will go well.
Miss the right time and things will go awry.

LIEH TZU

DECEMBER

The Wise do not value a huge gemstone as much as a little time. Time is hard to find and easy to lose.

LAO TZU

DECEMBER

When something enjoyable comes your way –
enjoy it completely!

LIEH TZU

DECEMBER

The Wise utterly devote themselves to everything in which they partake, every situation which contains them and within which they evolve.

CHUANG TZU

DECEMBER

The more creatively you live your life,
the more you will experience your essential nature.

LAO TZU

DECEMBER

The Wise witness events evolve,
yet keep to the Source.

LAO TZU

道生

DECEMBER

Those who follow Tao don't seek to arrive anywhere,
so their journey is never over.

LAO TZU

DECEMBER

Following Tao in the world
is like being a mountain stream
that becomes part of a valley brook,
which becomes part of a great river,
which flows to the one sea.

LAO TZU

DECEMBER

We are not alive for very long, so we should not put off listening to the inner voice of our heart.

LIEH TZU

DECEMBER

The way to nurture life
is through abstract thoughts and happy feelings.

LAO TZU

DECEMBER

Tao is not far away from where you are.
Those who go looking for it elsewhere
always return to here and now.

LAO TZU

DECEMBER

Be big hearted and friendly to everyone.
This is the highest teaching.

LAO TZU

DECEMBER

Be simple and true to your own nature.
Be selfless and at peace with the way things are.

LAO TZU

DECEMBER

Be quiet.
Look inside.
Soften your sharp edges.
Simplify your thoughts.
Follow your own light.
Be ordinary.
Then you will see for yourself
that you are a part of the Whole.

LAO TZU

DECEMBER

Just live and enjoy life.

LIEH TZU

DECEMBER

Mystified? Tao is mystery.
This is the gateway to understanding.

LAO TZU

INDEX

道牛

cupcakes
CW00890529

cupcakes

hamlyn

NOTES

Medium eggs have been used throughout.

A few recipes include nuts or nut derivatives. It is advisable for those with known allergic reactions to nuts and nut derivatives and those who may be potentially vulnerable to these allergies, such as pregnant and nursing mothers, invalids, the elderly, babies and children, to avoid dishes made with nuts and nut oils. It is also prudent to check the labels of prepared ingredients for the possible inclusion of nut derivatives.

Ovens should be preheated to the specified temperature. If using a convection oven, follow the manufacturer's instructions for adjusting the time and temperature.

An Hachette UK Company
www.hachette.co.uk

First published in Great Britain in 2004 by Hamlyn,
a division of Octopus Publishing Group Ltd
Endeavour House, 189 Shaftesbury Avenue,
London WC2H 8JY
www.octopusbooks.co.uk

This edition published in 2009

ISBN: 978-0-600-62145-4

A CIP catalogue record for this book is available from the British Library

Printed and bound in China

contents

introduction

Home-made cakes are always popular with family and friends, and cupcakes are no exception. Not only are they tasty and incredibly quick and easy to make, they also give you plenty of scope for decorating. They make ideal novelty cakes for kids' parties but are equally suitable for grown-up parties and for special family occasions like Christmas, Easter and Mother's Day.

Cupcakes keep well so you can make them in advance and keep a handy supply in the freezer or an airtight container until they're needed. If you really don't have time to make any you can even buy plain, undecorated cupcakes and decorate them yourself – within half an hour you can have a batch of beautifully presented cakes ready for guests or a hungry family.

Types of icing

Glacé icing The simplest glacé icing is made just with icing sugar and water beaten into a smooth icing. Alternatives include the use of orange or lemon juice instead of water, the addition of flavourings like instant coffee powder, or the use of food colouring to tint the icing. Use a thin glacé icing to coat the top of cakes, or add more icing sugar for a stiffer consistency and use it for decorative piping.

Buttercream The simplest recipe requires just icing sugar and butter. Like glacé icing, it can be coloured and/or flavoured with ingredients such as cocoa or instant coffee powder, lemon curd or finely grated citrus rind and can be used both for coating the tops of cupcakes and for decorative piping. It is very simple to make but can also be bought ready-made.

Rolled fondant This soft and smooth, easy-to-use commercial icing is available from cake decorating suppliers and some supermarkets. It usually comes in white, with a subtle flavour, but like the other icings can be easily coloured or flavoured by kneading it with food colouring or flavouring extracts. Rolled fondant can be rolled out and cut into flat shapes or moulded into fun 3D novelty decorations to put on top of cakes. Knead the rolled fondant before use to warm it up, then roll it out on a surface dusted with icing sugar and move it around frequently to keep it from sticking.

Writing icing Another ready-to-use commercial icing, writing icing comes in tubes with changeable tips for piping. Ideal for fun and speedy cake decorating, it is available in a variety of colours.

Decorating cupcakes

Decorating any cake is fun, but working with cupcakes is particularly satisfying since you can produce impressive results in virtually no time at all. The various home-made or commercial icings suitable for cupcakes can be coloured and used for topping the cakes, for decorative piping, or for modelling figures, but don't think such decorations restrict cupcakes to children. You can just as easily decorate cupcakes for special occasions like weddings (see page 32), or create cakes for a special afternoon tea party using whipped cream and thick custard as cake toppings instead of icing – see Espresso Cream Cakes (see page 58), Strawberry Cream Cakes (see page 52) and Praline Custard Cakes (see page 55).

There are a few decorating accessories and ingredients that you will find useful if you intend to do a lot of cupcakes decorating, although you may already have some items at home.

Piping bags and tips You can buy reusable nylon piping bags and large plastic 'syringes', both of which can be used with changeable tips. However, it is probably easier to use disposable paper piping bags for small-scale decorating. These can be bought ready-made from good cake decorating suppliers or you can easily make your own from triangles of greaseproof

paper. The advantage of disposable piping bags is that you can have several bags of icing in use at one time, whereas if you have only one reusable piping bag you will have to wash it out each time you want to change the colour or type of icing you are using. The two most useful tips for decorating cupcakes are the star tip, used for fancy lines and star shapes, and the plain tip, used for lines, dots and scribbling. Metal tips give better results than plastic ones.

Cookie cutters Made of metal or plastic, cookie cutters are invaluable for cutting out rolled fondant. They come in a variety of shapes – from simple round cutters to numerical and alphabetical shapes, animals, cars, hearts, stars, teddy bears and flowers, among many others. If you cannot find a cutter with the motif that you want, simply cut out the fondant freehand with a small sharp knife. Instead of a round pastry cutter you can use an upturned glass to cut out circles.

Food colouring Food colouring is available in liquid, gel and paste forms, and in many colours, although you can buy a few basic colours and mix them yourself to create other shades. They are quite concentrated so you need only a drop or two to colour icing. Transfer the colour to the icing on the end of a cocktail stick and mix well after each addition so that the colour is evenly distributed throughout, with no streaks. You can always add more colouring but it is difficult to rectify a case of over-colouring that results in an offputting blood red or navy blue icing!

Edible cake decorations Besides the huge range of small sweets suitable for decorating cupcakes – such as candy-coated chocolate drops, chocolate buttons, mini Easter eggs, wine gums and jelly beans – there are specialist edible decorations for cakes. Edible silver or gold balls, known as dragees, are small sugar balls with a coating of edible silver or gold leaf, while sugar strands are available in different sizes and various colours and flavours. Other specialist products include rice paper flowers and chocolate and coloured sprinkles. You can also buy chocolate curls or make your own by paring off 'ribbons' from a bar of softened chocolate with a vegetable peeler.

150 g (5 oz) **unsalted butter** or **margarine**, softened

150 g (5 oz) **caster sugar**

175 g (6 oz) **self-raising flour**

3 **eggs**

1 teaspoon **vanilla extract**

Vanilla cupcakes

1 Line a 12-section bun tray with paper cake cases. Put all the cake ingredients in a mixing bowl and beat with a hand-held electric whisk for 1–2 minutes until light and creamy. Divide the mixture evenly among the cake cases.

2 Bake in a preheated oven, 180°C (350°F), Gas Mark 4, for 18–20 minutes until risen and just firm to the touch. Transfer to a wire rack to cool.

Makes 12
Preparation time: 10 minutes
Cooking time: 18–20 minutes

VARIATIONS

Chocolate:
Substitute 15 g (½ oz) cocoa powder for 15 g (½ oz) of the flour.

Chocolate Chip:
Add 50 g (2 oz) plain, milk or white chocolate chips.

Coffee:
Add 1 tablespoon espresso or strong coffee powder.

Lemon/Orange/Citrus:
Add the finely grated rind of 1 lemon or 1 small orange, or combine the rinds of ½ lemon and ½ orange.

Cranberry or Blueberry:
Add 75 g (3 oz) dried cranberries or blueberries, chopped if large.

Ginger:
Add 2 teaspoons ground ginger and use light muscovado sugar instead of caster sugar.

Sultana:
Add 75 g (3 oz) sultanas.

Carrot Cupcakes

125 g (4 oz) **unsalted butter** or **margarine**, softened

125 g (4 oz) **light muscovado sugar**

150 g (5 oz) **self-raising flour**

1 teaspoon **baking powder**

1 teaspoon **ground mixed spice**

75 g (3 oz) **ground almonds**

2 **eggs**

finely grated rind of ½ **orange**

150 g (5 oz) **carrots**, grated

50 g (2 oz) **sultanas**

1 Line a 12-section bun tray with paper cake cases. Put the butter, sugar, flour, baking powder, mixed spice, ground almonds, eggs and orange rind in a mixing bowl and beat with a hand-held electric whisk for 1–2 minutes until light and creamy.

2 Add the grated carrots and sultanas and stir in until evenly combined. Divide the mixture evenly among the cake cases.

3 Bake in a preheated oven, 180°C (350°F), Gas Mark 4, for 25 minutes until risen and just firm to the touch. Leave to cool in the bun tray.

Makes 12
Preparation time: 15 minutes
Cooking time: 25 minutes

VARIATION
Banana:
Replace the grated carrots and orange rind with 1 large banana, mashed until smooth.

150 g (5 oz) **unsalted butter** or **margarine**, softened

150 g (5 oz) **light muscovado sugar**

200 g (7 oz) **self-raising flour**

3 **eggs**

1 teaspoon **almond extract**

50 g (2 oz) **chopped mixed nuts**

75 g (3 oz) **mixed dried fruit**

Fruit and nut cupcakes

1 Line a 12-section bun tray with paper cake cases. Put the butter, sugar, flour, eggs and almond extract in a mixing bowl and beat with a hand-held electric whisk for 1–2 minutes until light and creamy.

2 Add the chopped nuts and dried fruit and stir in until evenly combined. Divide the mixture evenly among the cake cases.

3 Bake in a preheated oven, 180°C (350°F), Gas Mark 4, for 25 minutes until risen and just firm to the touch. Transfer to a wire rack to cool.

Makes 12

Preparation time: 10 minutes

Cooking time: 25 minutes

Buttercream

150 g (5 oz) **unsalted butter**, softened

250 g (8 oz) **icing sugar**

1 teaspoon **vanilla extract**

2 teaspoons **hot water**

1 Put the butter and icing sugar in a bowl and beat well with a wooden spoon or hand-held electric whisk until smooth and creamy.

2 Add the vanilla extract and hot water and beat again until smooth.

Makes enough to cover 12 cupcakes
Preparation time: 5 minutes

VARIATIONS

Chocolate:
Mix 2 tablespoons cocoa powder with 2 tablespoons boiling water and use instead of the vanilla extract and hot water.

Citrus:
Add the finely grated rind of 1 orange or lemon.

Cream cheese frosting

125 g (4 oz) **cream cheese**

175 g (6 oz) **icing sugar**

1 tablespoon **lemon juice**

1 Beat the cream cheese in a bowl until smooth and creamy. Add the icing sugar and lemon juice and beat until completely smooth.

Makes enough to cover 12 cupcakes
Preparation time: 5 minutes

Chocolate fudge frosting

100 g ($3^1/_2$ oz) **plain** or **milk chocolate**, chopped

2 tablespoons **milk**

50 g (2 oz) **unsalted butter**

75 g (3 oz) **icing sugar**

1 Put the chocolate, milk and butter in a small, heavy-based saucepan and heat gently, stirring until the chocolate and butter have melted.

2 Remove from the heat and stir in the icing sugar until smooth. Spread the frosting over the tops of cupcakes while still warm.

Makes enough to cover 12 cupcakes
Preparation time: 5 minutes

White chocolate fudge frosting

200 g (7 oz) **white chocolate**, chopped

5 tablespoons **milk**

175 g (6 oz) **icing sugar**

1 Put the chocolate and milk in a heatproof bowl, set over a saucepan of gently simmering water and leave until melted, stirring frequently.

2 Remove the bowl from the pan and stir in the icing sugar until smooth. Spread the frosting over the tops of cupcakes while still warm.

Makes enough to cover 12 cupcakes
Preparation time: 5 minutes

2 tablespoons **strawberry** or **raspberry jam**

12 **cupcakes** (see pages 10–12)

175 g (6 oz) **green ready-to-roll icing**

icing sugar, for dusting

4 **flaked chocolate bars**, cut into 5 cm (2 inch) lengths

50 g (2 oz) **red ready-to-roll icing**

50 g (2 oz) **yellow ready-to-roll icing**

50 g (2 oz) **white ready-to-roll icing**

25 g (1 oz) **black ready-to-roll icing**

Snakes in the jungle

As long as you have green icing for the cake bases, you can make the snakes in any colours you like. Orange can easily be made by blending red and yellow icing, and pink by blending red and white.

1 Using a pastry brush, brush jam over the top of each cupcake. Knead the green ready-to-roll icing on a surface lightly dusted with icing sugar. Roll out very thinly and cut out 12 circles using a 6 cm (2½ inch) round cookie cutter. Place a green circle on top of each cake.

2 To shape a snake, take a small ball of ready-to-roll icing – about 7 g (¼ oz) – and roll under the palm of the hand to a thin sausage about 12–15 cm (5–6 inches) long, tapering it to a point at one end and shaping a head at the other. Flatten the head slightly and mark a mouth with a small, sharp knife.

3 Thinly roll a little ready-to-roll icing in a contrasting colour and cut out small diamond shapes. Secure along the snake using a dampened paintbrush. Wrap the snake around a length of flaked chocolate and position on top of a cake.

4 Make more snakes in the same way, kneading small amounts of the coloured ready-to-roll icing together to make different colours. For some of the cakes, press the chocolate bar vertically into the cake.

5 To make the snakes' eyes, roll small balls of white icing and press tiny balls of black icing over them. Secure to the snakes' heads with a dampened paintbrush.

Makes 12

Decoration time: 45 minutes

2 tablespoons **raspberry** or **strawberry jam**

12 **cupcakes** (see pages 10–12)

175 g (6 oz) **red ready-to-roll icing**

icing sugar, for dusting

125 g (4 oz) **black ready-to-roll icing**

15 g (½ oz) **white ready-to-roll icing**

small piece of **candied orange peel**, cut into matchstick lengths

Ladybirds

Thin strips of candied orange peel are used for the antennae on these little bugs. If you cannot get candied orange peel use small chocolate sticks instead.

1 Using a pastry brush, brush jam over the top of each cupcake. Knead the red ready-to-roll icing on a surface lightly dusted with icing sugar. Roll out very thinly and cut out 12 circles using a 6 cm (2½ inch) round cookie cutter. Place a red circle on top of each cake.

2 Roll out thin strips of black ready-to-roll icing and position one across each red circle, securing with a dampened paintbrush. Roll out half the remaining black icing to a thin sausage shape, about 1 cm (½ inch) in diameter. Cut into very thin slices and secure to the cakes to represent ladybird spots.

3 From the remaining black icing make oval-shaped heads and secure in position. Roll small balls of the white ready-to-roll icing for eyes and press tiny balls of black icing over them. Secure with a dampened paintbrush.

4 To make the ladybirds' antennae, press the lengths of candied orange peel into position behind the heads, pressing small balls of black icing on to their ends. Use tiny pieces of white icing to shape smiling mouths.

Makes 12

Decoration time: 30 minutes

Sea monster

1 quantity **Buttercream** (see page 13)

blue and **green food colourings**

12 **cupcakes** (see pages 10–12)

375 g (12 oz) **green ready-to-roll icing**

icing sugar, for dusting

15 g (½ oz) **red ready-to-roll icing**

2 red 'dots' **gumdrops**

15 g (½ oz) **black ready-to-roll icing**

1 Divide the buttercream between 2 bowls. Colour one half with the blue food colouring and the other with the green. Using a small palette knife, swirl the blue buttercream over a large flat platter or tray.

2 Remove one cake from its paper case and slice off the base at an angle so the top of the cake can be arranged over another at an angle to make the monster's face.

3 Spread the green buttercream over the tops of the 11 cakes in their cases. Place the cut cake on top of one of them and spread this with buttercream, too. Arrange the cakes on the blue buttercream base in a snaking line with the 'face' cake at the front.

4 Knead the green ready-to-roll icing on a surface lightly dusted with icing sugar. Roll out 125 g (4 oz) of the icing, keeping the rest wrapped in clingfilm, and cut out circles using a 7 cm (3 inch) round cookie cutter. Cut the circles in half and position each semicircle, upright, on the 9 centre cakes. Use a little more icing to shape a small pointed tail and secure to the cake at the end.

5 For the legs, divide the reserved green icing into 4 pieces. Shape each into a sausage, flatten the end and cut out claw shapes. Secure around the cakes, bending them so the claws face forward.

6 Roll the green icing trimmings and a little red icing together until marbled. Shape horns and secure to the monster's head. Position the sweets for eyes, then finish the eyes and add a mouth with a little black ready-to-roll icing.

Makes 1 'monster' cake of 12 cupcakes
Decoration time: 20 minutes

½ quantity **Buttercream** (see page 13)

12 **cupcakes** (see pages 10–12)

100 g (3½ oz) **brown ready-to-roll icing**

icing sugar, for dusting

100 g (3½ oz) **yellow ready-to-roll icing**

100 g (3½ oz) **pink ready-to-roll icing**

15 g (½ oz) **white ready-to-roll icing**

15 g (½ oz) **black ready-to-roll icing**

black food colouring

On the farm

1 Using a palette knife, spread a thick layer of the buttercream over 4 of the cakes and lightly peak. Spread the rest of the buttercream over the remaining cakes.

2 To make the sheep, take 75 g (3 oz) of the brown ready-to-roll icing, wrapping the remainder in clingfilm. Knead the icing on a surface lightly dusted with icing sugar. Reserve a small piece for the ears and roll the remainder into 4 balls. Flatten each ball into an oval shape and gently press on to the cakes thickly spread with buttercream. Shape and position small ears on each sheep.

3 To make the cows, reserve a small piece of the yellow ready-to-roll icing for the ears. Roll the remainder into 4 balls and flatten into oval shapes as large as the cake tops. Gently press on to 4 more cakes. Shape and position the ears. Use the remaining brown ready-to-roll icing to shape the cows' nostrils and horns, securing with a dampened paintbrush.

4 To make the pigs, reserve 25 g (1 oz) of the pink ready-to-roll icing for the snouts and ears. Roll the remainder into 4 balls and flatten into rounds, almost as large as each cake top. Shape and position the snouts and floppy ears, pressing 2 small holes in each snout with the tip of a cocktail stick or fine skewer.

5 Use the white and black icing to make all the animals' eyes – their shape and size to suit each animal. Roll small balls of white icing and press tiny balls of black icing over them. Secure with a dampened paintbrush.

6 Use a fine paintbrush, dipped in the black food colouring, to paint on additional features.

Makes 12

Decoration time: 45 minutes

1 quantity **Buttercream** (see page 13)

blue food colouring

12 **cupcakes** (see pages 10–12)

25 g (1 oz) **blue ready-to-roll icing**

25 g (1 oz) **red ready-to-roll icing**

25 g (1 oz) **green ready-to-roll icing**

50 g (2 oz) **yellow ready-to-roll icing**

icing sugar, for dusting

50 g (2 oz) **white ready-to-roll icing**

Rainbow cakes

1 Colour the buttercream with the blue food colouring and spread it all over the tops of the cupcakes using a small palette knife.

2 To make the rainbows, take 15 g (½ oz) of the blue, red, green and yellow icing and roll each piece under the palms of the hands on a surface lightly dusted with icing sugar until about 40 cm (16 inches) long. Push the strips together and then lightly roll with a rolling pin to flatten them and secure together.

3 Cut into 6 pieces, roughly 7 cm (3 inches) long, and secure to half the cakes, bending them into rainbow shapes and trimming off any excess around the edges. Reserve 25 g (1 oz) of the remaining yellow icing, then use all the leftover coloured icing to make another 6 rainbows for the rest of the cakes in the same way.

4 Thinly roll out the white icing and cut out little clouds. Secure to half the cakes.

5 To make the sun, thinly roll the remaining yellow icing and cut out 6 x 4 cm (1½ inch) circles. Using the tip of a sharp knife cut out little triangles from around the edges to make points. Bend the points slightly to one side and position the suns on the remaining cakes.

Makes 12

Decoration time: 25 minutes

Princess cakes

If you can find them, use silver-coloured paper cake cases to make these little cupcakes even more fit for a princess.

1 quantity **Buttercream** (see page 13)

pink food colouring

12 **cupcakes** (see pages 10–12)

edible silver balls

1 Divide the buttercream between 2 bowls and add a few drops of pink food colouring to one bowl. Mix well to colour the buttercream. Using a small palette knife, spread the pink buttercream over the tops of the cupcakes to within 5 mm (¼ inch) of the edges, doming it up slightly in the centre.

2 Put half the white buttercream in a piping bag fitted with a writing nozzle and the remainder in a bag fitted with a star nozzle. Pipe lines, 1 cm (½ inch) apart, across the pink buttercream, then across in the other direction to make a diamond pattern.

3 Use the icing in the other bag to pipe little stars around the edges. Decorate the piped lines with silver balls.

Makes 12

Decoration time: 20 minutes

Number cakes

1 quantity **Buttercream** (see page 13)

green or **yellow food colouring**

12 **cupcakes** (see pages 10–12)

175 g (6 oz) **white ready-to-roll icing**

icing sugar, for dusting

50 g (2 oz) **red ready-to-roll icing**

50 g (2 oz) **blue ready-to-roll icing**

coloured **sugar strands**

These are quick and easy and a great party cake for younger children. You can cut out the numbers by hand using a sharp knife, or use small number cookie cutters. The numbers could simply run from 1 to 12, or could represent the ages of the party goers.

1 Colour the buttercream with green or yellow food colouring and spread all over the tops of the cupcakes using a small palette knife.

2 Knead the white ready-to-roll icing on a surface lightly dusted with icing sugar then roll out. Cut out 12 circles using a 6 cm (2½ inch) round cookie cutter and gently press one on to the top of each cake.

3 Roll out the red ready-to-roll icing and cut out half the numbers. Secure to the cakes with a dampened paintbrush. Use the blue ready-to-roll icing for the remaining numbers.

4 Lightly brush the edges of white icing with a dampened paintbrush and scatter over the sugar strands.

Makes 12

Decoration time: 15 minutes

1 quantity **Cream Cheese Frosting** (see page 13)

12 **Carrot Cupcakes** (see page 11)

15 g (½ oz) **white ready-to-roll icing**

75 g (3 oz) **red ready-to-roll icing**

handful of **small multi-coloured sweets**

icing sugar, for dusting

1 tube **green writing icing**

fine red **ribbon**, to decorate (optional)

Christmas stockings

Use any selection of the smallest sweets you can find to decorate these little cakes. Alternatively, use larger, soft sweets and chop them into small pieces. If you are making them for small children you might prefer to use Vanilla Cupcakes (see page 10) and spread them with Buttercream (see page 13).

1 Using a small palette knife, spread the frosting over the tops of the cupcakes, spreading it right to the edges.

2 Roll the white ready-to-roll icing and a tiny piece of the red ready-to-roll icing together on a work surface under your fingers so they twist together. Cut into 2 cm (¾ inch) lengths and bend one end of each length to make candy canes. You'll need about 24 altogether.

3 Pile several coloured sweets to one side on the top of each cake and tuck the candy canes among them.

4 Knead the remaining red icing on a surface lightly dusted with icing sugar. Roll out then cut out small stocking shapes using a sharp knife, making sure the top edge of each stocking is at least 2.5 cm (1 inch) wide. Lay the stocking shapes just over the sweet decorations. Use the green writing icing to pipe details on to the stockings.

5 If liked, tie a length of red ribbon around each paper cake case to decorate and finish with a bow.

Makes 12

Decoration time: 20 minutes

Christmas garland

Make the cakes a couple of days beforehand, or well in advance and freeze them, so all you have to do is assemble the garland up to 24 hours before serving. Use gold, silver, patterned or white paper cake cases.

6 tablespoons **apricot jam**

1 tablespoon **water**

24 **Fruit and Nut Cupcakes** (see page 12) or **Cranberry Cupcakes** (see page 10)

icing sugar, for dusting

bunch of **red grapes**, washed

bunch of **green grapes**, washed

3–4 **clementines**, halved

3–4 **figs**, halved

plenty of **bay leaf sprigs**

1 Press the jam through a sieve into a small saucepan and add the water. Heat gently until softened then spread in a thin layer over the tops of the cupcakes.

2 Arrange 15–16 of the cakes in a staggered circle on a round flat platter or tray, at least 35 cm (14 inches) in diameter. Using a small fine sieve or tea strainer dust the cakes on the platter with plenty of icing sugar.

3 Fold a piece of paper into 4 thicknesses then cut out a holly leaf shape, about 6 cm (2½ inches) long. Press a holly leaf paper template gently on the centre of 4 more cakes and dust lavishly with icing sugar. Carefully lift off the templates by sliding a knife under the paper to remove them without disturbing the icing sugar. Repeat on the remaining cakes. Arrange the cakes in a circle on top of the first layer.

4 Cut the grapes into small clusters. Tuck all the fruits into the gaps around the cakes and into the centre of the plate. Finish by arranging small sprigs of bay leaves around the fruits.

Makes 1 garland of 24 cupcakes
Decoration time: 15 minutes

100 g (3½ oz) **white ready-to-roll icing**

200 g (7 oz) **icing sugar**, plus extra for dusting

12 **cupcakes** (see pages 10–12)

½ quantity **Buttercream** (see page 13)

4–5 teaspoons **cold water**

25 g (1 oz) **desiccated coconut**

Christmas stars

These festive cakes look stunning on the Christmas tea table. If you have time, make the stars at least 2 hours in advance so they have firmed up before you decorate the cakes.

1 Knead the white ready-to-roll icing on a surface lightly dusted with icing sugar. Roll out thickly and cut out star shapes using a small star-shaped cookie cutter. Transfer to a baking sheet lined with nonstick baking parchment and leave to harden while decorating the cakes.

2 Using a small sharp knife, cut out a deep, cone-shaped centre from each cake. Fill the cavity in each cake with buttercream and position a cut-out cone on each with the crust side face down.

3 Mix the icing sugar in a bowl with the cold water until smooth – the icing should hold its shape but not be too firm. Carefully spread the icing over the cakes and scatter with desiccated coconut.

4 Gently press a star into the top of each cake and leave to set.

Makes 12

Decoration time: 25 minutes

Mini Christmas cakes

12 **Fruit and Nut Cupcakes** (see page 12)

4 tablespoons **brandy** or **orange-flavoured liqueur** (optional)

2 tablespoons **apricot jam**

100 g (3½ oz) **ground hazelnuts** or **almonds**

50 g (2 oz) **caster sugar**

250 g (8 oz) **icing sugar**, plus extra for dusting

yellow food colouring

1 tablespoon **egg white**

4–5 teaspoons **cold water**

25 g (1 oz) **green ready-to-roll icing**

25 g (1 oz) **red ready-to-roll icing**

1 Drizzle the cupcakes with the liqueur, if using. Spread ½ teaspoon jam on to the centre of each cake.

2 To make the marzipan, put the ground nuts, caster sugar, 50 g (2 oz) of the icing sugar and a few drops of yellow food colouring in a bowl. Add the egg white and mix with a round-bladed knife until the mixture starts to cling together. Finish mixing the paste by hand until smooth and very firm. Lightly knead the marzipan and shape into a thick sausage, 7.5 cm (3½ inches) long. Cut into 12 thin slices and place a slice on top of each cake.

3 Put the remaining icing sugar in a bowl and add the cold water to make a thick smooth paste – the icing should hold its shape but not feel too firm. Gently spread the icing over the marzipan.

4 Use the green and red ready-to-roll icing to make small holly leaves and berries. Use to decorate the tops of the cakes.

Makes 12

Decoration time: 30 minutes

Love hearts

Make these as a family treat for Valentine's Day. Use Cream Cheese Frosting (see page 13) or White Chocolate Fudge Frosting (see page 14) instead of the glacé icing if preferred.

200 g (7 oz) **icing sugar**

4–5 teaspoons **rosewater** or **lemon juice**

12 **cupcakes** (see pages 10–12)

100 g (3½ oz) **red ready-to-roll icing**

icing sugar, for dusting

6 tablespoons **strawberry jam**

1 Put the icing sugar in a bowl and add 4 teaspoons of the rosewater or lemon juice. Mix until smooth, adding a little more liquid if necessary, until the icing is a thick paste. Spread over the tops of the cupcakes.

2 Knead the red ready-to-roll icing on a surface lightly dusted with icing sugar. Roll out thickly and cut out 12 heart shapes using a small heart-shaped cookie cutter. Place a heart on the top of each cake.

3 Press the jam through a small sieve to remove any seeds or pulp. Put the sieved jam in a small piping bag fitted with a writing nozzle. Pipe small dots into the icing around the edges of each cake and pipe a line of jam around the edges of the heart.

Makes 12

Decoration time: 20 minutes

12 **Vanilla Cupcakes** (see page 10)

4 tablespoons **sherry** or **orange-flavoured liqueur** (optional)

200 g (7 oz) **icing sugar**, sifted

1–2 tablespoons **lemon juice**

36 **sugared almonds**

12 **frosted flowers** (see page 43)

fine white **ribbon**, to decorate

Wedding cupcakes

Prettily decorated with sugared almonds, these little cakes are perfect for a country-style family wedding. You could add guests' name tags to them and place them around the dining table. Choose sugared almonds to suit the colour scheme of the wedding. If using ribbon, secure it around the paper cases before you begin decorating.

1 Drizzle the cakes with the liqueur, if using. Mix the icing sugar in a bowl with 1 tablespoon of the lemon juice. Gradually add the remaining lemon juice, stirring well with a wooden spoon until the icing holds its shape but is not difficult to spread – you might not need all the juice.

2 Spread the lemon-flavoured icing over the tops of the cupcakes using a small palette knife and arrange 3 sugared almonds in the centre of each.

3 Place a frosted flower on top of each cake and tie a length of white ribbon around each paper cake case to decorate it, finishing it with a bow.

Makes 12

Decoration time: 20 minutes

1 quantity **Chocolate Buttercream** (see page 13) or **Chocolate Fudge Frosting** (see page 14)

12 **Chocolate Cupcakes** (see page 10)

200 g (7 oz) **flaked chocolate bars**, cut into 2.5 cm (1 inch) lengths

36 candy-covered **chocolate mini eggs**

Easter nests

1 Using a small palette knife, spread the buttercream or chocolate icing over the tops of the cupcakes, spreading the mixture right to the edges.

2 Cut the short lengths of flaked chocolate bars lengthways into thin 'shards'.

3 Arrange the chocolate shards around the edges of the cakes, pressing them into the icing at different angles to resemble birds' nests. Pile 3 eggs into the centre of each 'nest'.

Makes 12

Decoration time: 20 minutes

1 quantity **Buttercream** (see page 13)

yellow and **blue food colourings**

12 **cupcakes** (see pages 10–12)

2 **glacé cherries**

Ducks, bunnies and chicks

1 Put two-thirds of the buttercream in a bowl, beat in a few drops of yellow food colouring and mix well. Using a small palette knife, spread the yellow icing in a flat layer over the tops of the cupcakes.

2 Colour the remaining buttercream with blue food colouring. Place in a piping bag fitted with a writing nozzle, or use a greaseproof paper piping bag with the tip snipped off.

3 Pipe simple duck, bunny and chick shapes on to the iced cakes. Cut the glacé cherries into thin slices, then into tiny triangles and use to represent beaks on the ducks and chicks, and tiny eyes on the bunnies.

Makes 12

Decoration time: 25 minutes

300 g (10 oz) **icing sugar**

2 tablespoons **cold water**

black and **red food colourings**

12 **cupcakes** (see pages 10–12)

12 **jelly insect sweets**

Spiders' webs

For best results, finish decorating one cake before moving on to the next as the icing must be really soft to make the web patterns work well. Use any selection of sweet insects – either the spiders or the bugs can be caught in the web!

1 Beat the icing sugar in a bowl with the cold water until smooth – the icing should be soft enough to lose its shape when the spoon is lifted from the bowl. If necessary add a dash more water.

2 Transfer one-quarter of the icing to a separate bowl and stir in a little black food colouring. Put in a piping bag fitted with a writing nozzle.

3 Colour the remaining icing red. Drop 1 teaspoonful of the red icing on to a cake and spread it to the edges. Starting at the edges of the cake, pipe a spiral of black icing that finishes in the centre of the cake. Run the tip of a cocktail stick or fine skewer from the centre of the spiral out to the edge. Repeat at intervals around the cake to make a spider's web pattern, then decorate with a jelly insect.

4 Repeat on all the remaining cupcakes.

Makes 12

Decoration time: 25 minutes

Flying bats

125 g (4 oz) **black ready-to-roll icing**

icing sugar, for dusting

2 tablespoons **clear honey**

12 **cupcakes** (see pages 10–12)

175 g (6 oz) **orange ready-to-roll icing**

1 tube **black writing icing**

selection of tiny red, orange and yellow **sweets**

1 Knead the black ready-to-roll icing on a surface lightly dusted with icing sugar. Roll out thickly and cut out 12 bat shapes by hand or using a small bat-shaped cookie cutter. Transfer to a baking sheet lined with nonstick baking parchment and leave to harden while decorating the cakes.

2 Spread ½ teaspoon honey over the top of each cupcake. Thinly roll out the orange ready-to-roll icing and cut out circles using a 6 cm (2½ inch) round cookie cutter. Place an orange circle on top of each cake.

3 Place a bat on top of each cake. Dampen the edge of the orange icing and press the sweets gently into the icing. Pipe a wiggly line of black icing over the sweets.

Makes 12

Decoration time: 30 minutes

12 **Vanilla Cupcakes**
(see page 10)

1 quantity **Buttercream**
(see page 13)

Butterfly cakes

1 Using a small, sharp knife cut out the centre from each cake and slice each scooped-out piece in half.

2 Put the buttercream in a big piping bag fitted with a large star nozzle. Pipe a large swirl of icing into the hollow of each cake.

3 Reposition the cut-out centres on each cake at an angle of 45° so they resemble butterfly wings.

Makes 12

Decoration time: 15 minutes

7 tablespoons **raspberry** or **strawberry jam**

12 **Orange Cupcakes** (see page 10)

300 g (10 oz) **icing sugar**

2 tablespoons **orange juice**

Feather cakes

For these delicately patterned cakes, finish decorating one cake before starting on another as the icing quickly starts to set once spooned on to the cakes.

1 Press the jam through a sieve to remove any seeds or pulp. Put 3 tablespoons of the sieved jam into a small piping bag fitted with a writing nozzle and set aside. Spread the remaining jam over the tops of the cupcakes.

2 Put the icing sugar in a bowl and beat in the orange juice until smooth – the icing should be soft enough to lose its shape when the spoon is lifted from the bowl. If necessary add a few more drops of juice.

3 Spoon a thick layer of icing on to a cake and spread it to the edges. Using the jam in the piping bag, pile large dots of jam, 1 cm (½ inch) apart, on to the icing in a spiral, working from the edge of the cake to the centre. Draw the tip of a cocktail stick or fine skewer through the dots so they almost join up.

4 Repeat on the remaining cakes and leave to set.

Makes 12

Decoration time: 15 minutes

Frosted primrose cakes

These make a great gift for Mum – on Mother's Day or at any time during spring when flowers like primroses are at their best. Once frosted, the flowers keep for several weeks in a cool place so you can make them well in advance.

1 Make sure the flowers are clean and thoroughly dry before frosting. Put the egg white in a small bowl and the sugar in another.

2 Using your fingers or a soft brush, coat all the petals on both sides with egg white. Dust plenty of sugar over the flowers until evenly coated. Transfer to a sheet of nonstick baking parchment and leave for at least 1 hour until firm.

3 Using a small palette knife, spread the chocolate frosting over the tops of the cakes. Decorate the top of each with the frosted flowers. Tie a length of ribbon around each paper cake case to decorate and finish in a bow.

Makes 12

Decoration time: 30 minutes

selection of small **spring flowers** such as primroses, violets or rose petals

a little lightly beaten **egg white**

caster sugar, for dusting

1 quantity **White Chocolate Fudge Frosting** (see page 14)

12 **Vanilla Cupcakes** (see page 10)

fine pastel-coloured **ribbon**, to decorate

200 g (7 oz) **icing sugar**, plus a little extra

1–2 tablespoons **lemon** or **orange juice**

12 **cupcakes** (see pages 10–12)

½ quantity **Buttercream** (see page 13)

pink and **lilac food colourings**

Piped shell cakes

These are great fun for all the family to create – children love piping their own designs and personalizing cakes with names or messages. The pink and lilac piping looks pretty on the white background but you can choose any mixture of colours you like.

1 Mix the icing sugar in a bowl with 1 tablespoon of the lemon or orange juice. Gradually add the remaining juice, stirring well with a wooden spoon until the icing holds its shape but is not difficult to spread. You might not need all the juice.

2 Reserve 3 tablespoons of the icing and spread the remainder over the tops of the fairy cakes using a small palette knife. Stir a little extra icing sugar into the reserved icing to thicken it until it just forms peaks when lifted with a knife. Put in a piping bag fitted with a writing nozzle.

3 Colour half the buttercream with pink food colouring and the other half with lilac. Place in separate piping bags fitted with star nozzles.

4 Pipe rows of pink, lilac and white icing across some of the cakes.

Makes 12

Decoration time: 30 minutes

1 quantity **Cream Cheese Frosting** (see page 13) or **Buttercream** (see page 13)

12 **cupcakes** (see pages 10–12)

selection of **small sweets**, such as mini mallows, gumdrops or jelly beans

Candy cakes

To make these cakes really effective stick to the same shades of colour throughout for the sweet decorations – either pastels or shocking colours – combining 2 or 3 different types of sweets. These are great fun for children to decorate.

1 Using a small palette knife, spread the frosting or buttercream over the tops of the cupcakes.

2 Decorate each cake by sprinkling with a thick, even layer of small sweets.

Makes 12

Decoration time: 10 minutes

Stars, spots and stripes

½ quantity **Buttercream** (see page 13)

12 **cupcakes** (see pages 10–12)

150 g (5 oz) **white ready-to-roll icing**

125 g (4 oz) **blue ready-to-roll icing**

icing sugar, for dusting

1 Using a small palette knife, spread the buttercream in a thin layer over the tops of the cakes.

2 Knead the ready-to-roll icings on a surface lightly dusted with icing sugar, keeping the colours separate. Take 50 g (2 oz) of the white icing, roll out thinly and cut out 4 circles using a 6 cm (2½ inch) round cookie cutter. Cut out 6 small stars from each circle using a tiny star-shaped cutter. Thinly roll out a little of the blue icing and cut out stars. Fit the blue stars into each white round and carefully transfer to 4 of the cakes.

3 Thinly roll out another 50 g (2 oz) of the white icing. Roll balls of blue icing, about the size of a small pea, between the finger and thumb. Press at intervals on to the white icing. Gently roll with a rolling pin so the blue icing forms dots over the white. Cut out 4 circles using the round cookie cutter and transfer to 4 more of the cakes.

4 From the remaining blue and white icing cut out long strips 5 mm (¼ inch) wide and lay them together on the work surface to make stripes. Roll lightly with a rolling pin to flatten them and secure together, then cut out 4 more circles. Place on top of the remaining 4 cakes.

Makes 12
Decoration time: 20 minutes

200 g (7 oz) (about ½ can) **sweetened condensed milk**

50 g (2 oz) **caster sugar**

65 g (2½ oz) **unsalted butter**

2 tablespoons **golden syrup**

12**cupcakes** (see pages 10–12)

100 g (3½ oz) **plain chocolate**, chopped

100 g (3½ oz) **milk chocolate**, chopped

Chocolate toffee cupcakes

1 Put the condensed milk, sugar, butter and golden syrup in a medium heavy-based saucepan and heat gently, stirring, until the sugar dissolves. Cook over a gentle heat, stirring, for about 5 minutes until the mixture has turned a pale fudge colour.

2 Leave to cool for 2 minutes then spoon the toffee over the top of the cupcakes.

3 Melt the plain and milk chocolate in separate heatproof bowls, either one at a time in the microwave or by resting each bowl over a saucepan of gently simmering water. Place a couple of teaspoons of each type of melted chocolate on to a cake, mixing up the colours and tap the cake on the work surface to level the chocolate.

4 Using the tip of a cocktail stick or fine skewer, swirl the chocolates together to marble them lightly. Repeat on the remaining cakes.

Makes 12

Cooking time: 5 minutes

Decoration time: 15 minutes

50 g (2 oz) **unsalted butter**

50 g (2 oz) **caster sugar**

2 tablespoons **golden syrup**

100 g (3½ oz) **crispy rice breakfast cereal**

12 **cupcakes** (see pages 10–12)

icing sugar, for dusting

Toffee crisp pyramids

1 Put the butter, sugar and golden syrup in a medium heavy-based saucepan and heat gently until the sugar dissolves. Cook the mixture for 2–3 minutes until it is pale toffee coloured, stirring frequently. Immerse the base of the pan in cold water to prevent further cooking.

2 Stir in the crispy rice breakfast cereal and mix until evenly coated. Pile a little of the mixture on to the top of each cupcake and shape into a pyramid. Leave until cold then lightly dust the tops with icing sugar.

Makes 12

Cooking time: 5 minutes

Decoration time: 10 minutes

Tee-off cakes

Golf-crazy Dads will love these little cupcakes, particularly if you get the children involved with the decoration. If you cannot find chocolate 'golf balls', you can easily shape some out of white ready-to-roll icing and make the golf ball-like impressions with the tip of a blunt-ended paintbrush.

1 Beat the chocolate spread or icing to soften it slightly then spread it over the tops of the fairy cakes using a small palette knife.

2 Knead the green ready-to-roll icing on a surface lightly dusted with icing sugar. Roll out thinly and cut out 12 circles using a 5 cm (2 inch) round cookie cutter. Place a green circle on top of each cake.

3 Use the white ready-to-roll icing to shape 12 small golf tees. Lay one on top of each cake, securing with a dampened paintbrush. Press a foil-wrapped chocolate golf ball into the icing, alongside the tee, to finish.

Makes 12

Decoration time: 30 minutes

8 tablespoons **chocolate hazelnut spread** or ½ quantity **Chocolate Fudge Frosting** (see page 14)

12 **cupcakes** (see pages 10–12)

200 g (7 oz) **green ready-to-roll icing**

icing sugar, for dusting

75 g (3 oz) **white ready-to-roll icing**

12 **foil-wrapped chocolate golf balls**

12 **Vanilla Cupcakes** (see page 10)

300 g (10 oz) small **strawberries**

150 ml (¼ pint) **double cream**

2 teaspoons **caster sugar**

½ teaspoon **vanilla extract**

4 tablespoons **redcurrant jelly**

1 tablespoon **water**

Strawberry cream cakes

1 Using a small sharp knife, scoop out the centre of each cupcake to leave each cake with a deep cavity. Reserve 6 of the smallest strawberries and thinly slice the remainder.

2 Using a hand-held electric whisk, whip the cream with the sugar and vanilla extract until just peaking. Spoon a little into the centre of each cake and flatten slightly with the back of the spoon.

3 Arrange the sliced strawberries, overlapping, around the edges of each cake. Halve the reserved strawberries and place a strawberry half in the centre of each cake.

4 Heat the redcurrant jelly in a small heavy-based saucepan with the water until melted, then brush over the strawberries using a pastry brush. Store the cakes in a cool place until ready to serve.

Makes 12

Decoration time: 20 minutes

3 small **oranges**

100 g (3½ oz) **caster sugar**

300 ml (½ pint) **water**

12 **Citrus Cupcakes** (see page 10)

Candied orange cupcakes

This recipe uses whole orange slices, including the skins. Cooked in syrup over a very low heat, they turn meltingly soft and delicious.

1 Slice the oranges as thinly as possible and discard any pips. Put the sugar in a medium heavy-based saucepan with the water and heat very gently, stirring with a wooden spoon, until the sugar dissolves.

2 Add the orange slices and reduce the heat to its lowest setting. Cover the saucepan and cook very gently for about 50–60 minutes or until the orange slices are thoroughly tender.

3 Transfer the slices to a plate using a slotted spoon and leave to cool slightly. Boil the syrup left in the saucepan until it is very thick and syrupy. Leave to cool for 5 minutes.

4 Arrange the orange slices over the cupcakes. Brush the thickened syrup over the cakes and leave to cool completely.

Makes 12

Cooking time: 50–60 minutes

Decoration time: 10 minutes

Praline custard cakes

100 g (3½ oz) **caster sugar**

100 ml (3½ fl oz) **water**

50 g (2 oz) **unblanched hazelnuts**, chopped

12 **Vanilla Cupcakes** (see page 10)

300 ml (½ pint) good-quality **creamy custard**

When making the caramel for these cakes, watch the saucepan closely towards the end of the cooking time. You want the caramel to be deep golden in colour but not too dark as the sugar will start to burn and taste bitter.

1 To make the caramel, put the sugar in a small heavy-based saucepan with the water. Heat gently, stirring with a wooden spoon, until the sugar has dissolved. Bring to the boil and boil rapidly for about 10 minutes, until the syrup has turned a golden caramel.

2 Immediately remove the pan from the heat and immerse the base in cold water for a few seconds to prevent further cooking. Stir in the nuts and tip the mixture on to a lightly oiled large baking sheet, spreading it in a thin layer. Leave for about 20 minutes until brittle.

3 Scoop out and discard the centre from each cupcake using a teaspoon. Break the nut brittle in half and place one half in a polythene bag. Tap gently with a rolling pin until the brittle is broken into small chunks. Turn out on to a plate then put the remaining brittle in the bag. Beat firmly with the rolling pin until the brittle is finely crushed.

4 Mix the crushed brittle with the custard and pile the mixture into the cakes. Decorate with the large pieces of brittle.

Makes 12

Cooking time: 10 minutes, plus cooling

Decoration time: 15 minutes

75 g (3 oz) **flaked almonds**

50 g (2 oz) **sultanas**

125 g (4 oz) **glacé cherries**, quartered

4 tablespoons **golden syrup**

12 **cupcakes** (see pages 10–12)

50 g (2 oz) **plain chocolate**, broken into pieces

Florentine cupcakes

1 Mix together the flaked almonds, sultanas, glacé cherries and golden syrup in a bowl. Tip the mixture out on to a greased baking sheet and spread in a thin layer. Bake in a preheated oven, 200°C (400°F), Gas Mark 6, for 8 minutes or until the nuts and syrup are turning golden. Remove from the oven and leave to cool slightly.

2 Break up the mixture and scatter over the cakes in an even layer.

3 Melt the chocolate in a heatproof bowl, either in the microwave or by resting the bowl over a saucepan of gently simmering water. Put the melted chocolate in a piping bag fitted with a writing nozzle. Scribble lines of chocolate across the fruit and nut topping. Leave to set.

Makes 12
Cooking time: 8 minutes
Decoration time: 10 minutes

12 **Coffee Cupcakes** (see page 10)

4 tablespoons **coffee-flavoured liqueur**

300 ml (½ pint) **double cream**

75 g (3 oz) piece of **plain** or **milk chocolate**

cocoa or **drinking chocolate powder**, for sprinkling

Espresso cream cakes

These richly flavoured cakes make a delicious treat with morning coffee. If you don't want to use the liqueur, use 4 tablespoons of strong black coffee mixed with 1 teaspoon of sugar instead.

1 Flavour the cupcakes by drizzling with 2 tablespoons of the coffee liqueur.

2 Put the remaining liqueur in a bowl with the cream and whip with a hand-held electric whisk until the cream is thickened and only just holds its shape. Using a small palette knife, spread the cream over the tops of the cupcakes, swirling it right to the edges.

3 Using a vegetable peeler, pare off curls from the chocolate bar – if the chocolate breaks off in small, brittle shards, try softening it in the microwave for a few seconds first, but take care not to overheat and melt it. Scatter the chocolate curls over the cakes and sprinkle with a little cocoa or drinking chocolate powder. Store the cakes in a cool place until ready to serve.

Makes 12

Decoration time: 10 minutes

Chocolate truffle cakes

200 g (7 oz) **plain chocolate**

150 ml (¼ pint) **double cream**

12 **Chocolate Cupcakes** (see page 10)

24 **cocoa-dusted chocolate truffles**, quartered

1 Coarsely grate 50 g (2 oz) of the chocolate and set aside. Chop the remainder into pieces.

2 Heat the cream in a small heavy-based saucepan until just beginning to bubble around the edges. Remove from the heat and add the chopped chocolate. Leave to stand for a few minutes until the chocolate has melted.

3 Turn the mixture into a bowl and leave to cool until the cream just holds its shape – you can pop it in the refrigerator for a short while but don't leave it for too long as the mixture will eventually set.

4 Using a small palette knife, spread the chocolate cream over the tops of the cupcakes. Scatter the truffle quarters over the cakes. Sprinkle with the grated chocolate and leave the cakes in a cool place until ready to serve.

Makes 12

Decoration time: 15 minutes

100 g (3½ oz) chunky piece of **white chocolate**

1 quantity **White Chocolate Fudge Frosting** (see page 14)

12 **White Chocolate Chip Cupcakes** (see page 10)

icing sugar, for dusting

White chocolate curl cakes

1 Using a vegetable peeler, pare off curls from the chocolate bar – if the chocolate breaks off in small, brittle shards, try softening it in the microwave for a few seconds first, but take care not to overheat and melt it. Set the chocolate curls aside in a cool place while icing the cakes.

2 Using a small palette knife, spread the fudge frosting all over the tops of the cupcakes.

3 Pile the chocolate curls on to the fairy cakes and lightly dust with icing sugar.

Makes 12

Decoration time: 15 minutes

100 g (3½ oz) **white chocolate**, chopped

100 g (3½ oz) **milk chocolate**, chopped

100 g (3½ oz) **plain chocolate**, chopped

40 g (1½ oz) **unsalted butter**

12 **Chocolate Cupcakes** (see page 10)

cocoa powder, for dusting

Triple chocolate cupcakes

1 Put the white, milk and plain chocolate in separate bowls and add 15 g (½ oz) butter to each. Melt all the chocolate, either one at a time in the microwave or by resting each bowl over a saucepan of gently simmering water. Stir occasionally until melted and smooth.

2 Using a small palette knife, spread the melted white chocolate over 4 of the cakes and sprinkle with a little cocoa powder.

3 Put 2 tablespoons of the melted milk and plain chocolate in separate piping bags fitted with writing nozzles. Spread the milk chocolate over 4 more of the cakes and pipe dots of plain chocolate over the milk chocolate.

4 Spread the plain chocolate over the 4 remaining cakes and scribble with lines of piped milk chocolate.

Makes 12

Decoration time: 20 minutes

Index

Executive Editor Sarah Ford
Managing Editor Clare Churly
Executive Art Editor Geoff Fennell
Photographer Gareth Sambidge
Food Stylist Joanna Farrow